He Is Coming Back

The Covenant Keeper

By Marah Saruchera

First Edition

Copyright © 10 April 2019 Marah Saruchera

Where biblical text is referenced, any one of the following
bible versions can be used:
King James Version
New King James Version
New International Version
Revised Standard Version

ISBN 978-1-77906-719-7

Book Design by:
Enhance Graphics
enhancegraphix@gmail.com

CONTENTS

PREFACE

Jesus came, so that we are fully and completely covered from the shame that nakedness brings. He came so that we are fully and completely covered by His blood.

The enemy's plan and purpose is to uncover us, and without the mercies of God we are exposed, it does not matter what we do and how we do it. We just need the Lord Himself to cover us.

This, our God, will tread upon every high thing that exalts itself against the knowledge of God. He will lift up everything that depends on and is sustained by His love. God will be God to those that will want to be His.

Our faith should be a pillar from which we can lean and magnify God. We can therefore not be careless about our faith.

Carelessness concerning the morals, the principles, the messages, the ethics, the standards and the meanings that we share and are credited to our lives. When we get careless with our faith, we are misunderstood and our lives do not mean what they are meant to mean. Our lives are supposed to reflect the power of the presence of the Lord.

Psalms 89:34 *My covenant will I not break, nor alter the thing that is gone out of my lips.*

When we get careless with our faith, we miss heaven.

The Bible says in Leviticus 18:3 *After the doings of the land of Egypt, **wherein ye dwelt,** shall ye not do: and after the doings of the land of Canaan, **whither I bring you,** shall ye not do: **neither shall ye walk in their ordinances.*** *⁴ Ye shall do my judgments, and keep mine ordinances, to walk therein: I am the* LORD *your God.*

Christianity is saying it, and living it. Jesus therefore came to stand in the breach, to reconcile us to the Father, because we kept doing what the Lord said we should not do, we were exposed.

Jesus will pluck out and pull out WHOSOEVER, from the sin gutters.

Jesus came and hung on the cross so that you and I can plead the blood of Jesus on our lives, and everything else that is ours.

The blood of Jesus washes whiter than snow. Jesus is the foundation of our faith. Jesus is the way to the Father. With and in Jesus, we have **THE BLOOD COVENANT – AN UNCHANGING COVENANT**

Psalms **89:34** *My covenant will I not break, nor alter the thing that is gone out of my lips.*

Introduction

There is a time in our lives when God seems far away, distant, an ideology, or even a myth.

There are also moments of doubt. Thomas said to the disciples who had seen Jesus whilst he was away – I want to see His hands – His palms. That was a moment of doubt, regardless of the fact that Thomas had been there when they almost had a ship wreck, and Jesus quieted the waters.

Thomas had been there when Jesus fed the multitudes, not once, but twice. Thomas was there when legion was redeemed, and Thomas was there when the dead Lazarus was raised.

Thomas was there all the time, but he doubted, even what Jesus had said to all of them.

Jesus had said He would be tried, would die but would rise from the dead.

Peter did not doubt, he was just afraid. How could he escape, how would he handle it if the multitude and the soldiers came for him. Peter was not ready for the challenge.

But Peter had walked on water.

Psalms 89:34 *My covenant will I not break, nor alter the thing that is gone out of my lips.*

Then John the Baptist had questions. The questions were so serious John the Baptist sent his disciples to verify.

Jesus answered, as quoted by Luke. *Then Jesus answering said unto them, Go your way, and tell John what things ye have seen and heard; how that the blind see, the lame walk, the lepers are cleansed, the deaf hear, the dead are raised, to the poor the gospel is preached.* **Luke 6:22**

What we believe makes the difference.

━━━ *Chapter 1* ━━━

Jesus Is Not An Ideology

God lives outside time yet very time conscious.

On the issues of God, your opinion and my opinion do not matter.

- **God's Law defines what is wrong and what is right.**
- **God's Word defines what is and what is not.**
- **God's Grace defines who is and who is not.**
- **The Blood of Jesus defines how it is and how it is not.**

In **John 14:15** Jesus says *If ye love me, keep my commandments.* This statement does not give room for our opinions, it is not a subject for discussion, and it is a statement from the word of God. The word spoken by

Psalms 89:34 *My covenant will I not break, nor alter the thing that is gone out of my lips.*

the Creator of the Universe, the Giver of Life, and life in all its forms.

John then says in **1 John 5:3** F*or this is the love of God, that we keep his commandments: and his commandments are not grievous.*

Love is a decision, it is not a feeling. God made a decision – to love you and to love me.

The Lord God gave us, human beings, one hundred and twenty years, or seventy to eighty, yet like David says in Psalms we are more precious than the whole universe. It could not be any other way, because the Bible says we were made in the image of God.

The image is not in the way we look, because we all look different from each other, some dark, some light, some short, some tall, some slim some plus sizes. No, the image cannot be in the way we look.

The image cannot be in the way we talk, because our tongues are a source of all sorts of conflicts, and it is not in the way we think – because our thoughts are impure, most of the time.

The image is not physical, neither is it social nor mental.

The image is spiritual.

Psalms 89:34 *My covenant will I not break, nor alter the thing that is gone out of my lips.*

This means there ought to be something more, something better, than what we see, what we hear, what we eat. There has to be something better – all way round.

Some lived close to a thousand years, the man of Genesis, but even for them, there ought to have been something better, something more.

The word of God is quick and powerful. It is true, yet it is so often not believed. Those that believe it have faith.

This faith is expecting the word of God to do what it says it will do, and depending on the word of God to do what it says it will do.

Nothing is neglected in the eyes of God. Everything the Lord does, is deliberate. To those who know Him, who love Him, who believe in and follow His Son, Jesus, God made and God makes the decisions.

What life has taught us is people say what their audience want or expect to hear. But Truth has really no agenda. All Truth, is in Jesus, it is in the word of God. Jesus is the word of God.

John says in **John 1** *In the beginning was the Word, and the Word was with God, and the Word was God. [2] The same was in the beginning with God. [3] All things were made by him; and without him was not any thing made that was made. [4] In him was life; and the life was the light of men.....[10] He was in the world, and the world was*

Psalms **89:34** *My covenant will I not break, nor alter the thing that is gone out of my lips.*

made by him, and the world knew him not. ¹¹ *He came unto his own, and his own received him not.* ¹² *But as many as received him, to them gave he power to become the sons of God, even to them that believe on his name:...* ¹⁴ *And the Word was made flesh, and dwelt among us, (and we beheld his glory, the glory as of the only begotten of the Father,) full of grace and truth.*

We expect to be told the truth, yet we avoid telling the truth. This does not matter whether it is to family, friends, teachers, pastors or neighbours. Truth is like water. Human beings can only live for a few days to possibly two weeks if completely deprived of water. Water, fresh and clean, is neutral. It is not acidic, it is not alkaline. The truth from the word of God, in my mind, is just like water, fresh and clean water.

Jesus is our example. He lived by the Truth. One cannot make an argument with the word of God. It is either one believes this word, or they reject it, but it remains The Truth.

This book is about the promises God made, statements which He spoke, deeds which we saw, which evidence that God is God. God sent His son Jesus, and Jesus did what He had to do, died, resurrected, went back to heaven and….. He is coming back!

God is a covenant keeper. The Bible says in **Numbers 23:19** *God is not a man, that he should lie; neither the*

***Psalms** 89:34 My covenant will I not break, nor alter the thing that is gone out of my lips.*

son of man, that he should repent: hath he said, and shall he not do it? or hath he spoken, and shall he not make it good?

In the book of Jeremiah the Bible says *Then said the LORD unto me, Thou hast well seen: for I will hasten my word to perform it.* **Jeremiah 1:12**

God is watching, to perform what He promised, what His word promised, so one day, some one very good day, Jesus is coming back to take His, to His Father.

The Bible describes this Jesus in **Isaiah 53:1-6**. Isaiah starts by asking – who shall believe our report. What report?

If the elders and the deacons, the scribes and the Pharisees, the Jews of that day, could not believe what they saw, what then can we do? Can we believe?

We have not seen Jesus in the physical, but have known Him in the spiritual. We have not touched Him,

yet we can and have touched the works of His hands.

So when Isaiah describes Jesus, it is not just for them in the synagogue, but to us too. And between us and them – who shall believe this story, (unless Christ is revealed to us), who can believe that this Jesus would *grow up ... as a tender plant, and as a root out of a dry ground: he would have no form nor comeliness; and when we shall*

Psalms 89:34 *My covenant will I not break, nor alter the thing that is gone out of my lips.*

see him, there is no beauty that we should desire him.
Isaiah 53:1-2

This Jesus, when all is well with us, we have no reason to desire Him.

The Bible says in **Isaiah 53:3** *He is despised and rejected of men; a man of sorrows, and acquainted with grief: and we hid as it were our faces from him; he was despised, and we esteemed him not.*

This was Jesus in the physical. Those that thronged to see Him wanted to see how He could heal, but they never accepted who He was.

Isaiah 53:4 says *Surely he hath borne our griefs, and carried our sorrows: yet we did esteem him stricken, smitten of God, and afflicted.*

We "pray" that someone, somewhere, bear the pain of our bad choices, we want the consequences of bad decisions somehow washed off, we want someone to just bear our burdens. This is what we want. Then Jesus says Come to Me!

So burdened, by illness, by poverty in all its forms, by famine, by death, we do not want to run to Jesus. Instead we ask Who are you? Or even Who are you Jesus?!

We ask Jesus to identify Himself. Really?

Psalms 89:34 *My covenant will I not break, nor alter the thing that is gone out of my lips.*

The Bible says in **John 1:15** *John bare witness of him, and cried, saying, This was he of whom I spake, He that cometh after me is preferred before me: **for he was before me.***

Jesus was before John the Baptist.

Jeremiah says in **Jeremiah 10:16** *The portion of Jacob is not like them: **for he is the former of all things;** and Israel is the rod of his inheritance: The LORD of hosts is his name.* (also **Jeremiah 51:19**)

This Jesus, Isaiah says *But he was wounded for our transgressions; he was bruised for our iniquities: the chastisement of our peace was upon him; and with his stripes we are healed. [6] All we like sheep have gone astray; we have turned everyone to his own way; and the LORD hath laid on him the iniquity of us all.* **Isaiah 53:5-6**

This Jesus Isaiah introduced in **Isaiah 9:6-7**. He says [6] *For unto us a child is born, unto us a son is given: and the government shall be upon his shoulder: and his name shall be called Wonderful, Counsellor, The mighty God, The everlasting Father, The Prince of Peace. [7] Of the increase of his government and peace there shall be no end.....*

This is the gospel of Jesus Christ.

Psalms 89:34 *My covenant will I not break, nor alter the thing that is gone out of my lips.*

Paul says to the Romans in **Romans 1:16** *For I am not ashamed of the gospel of Christ: for it is the power of God unto salvation to everyone that believeth; to the Jew first, and also to the Greek.*

That if thou shalt confess with thy mouth the Lord Jesus, and shalt believe in thine heart that God hath raised him from the dead, thou shalt be saved. [10] ***For with the heart man believeth unto righteousness; and with the mouth confession is made unto salvation.*** Romans 10:9-10

This, is the Truth.

***Psalms* 89:34** *My covenant will I not break, nor alter the thing that is gone out of my lips.*

━━━━ *Chapter 2* ━━━━

Faithful & True Sayings

John the Revelator, as John who wrote the book of Revelation is commonly called, talks a number of times about Jesus saying to him – write.

This was new. In the whole Bible, there are a few instances where **God instructed** someone to write. When it mattered, in the wilderness of Sinai, God wrote. And to Moses God instructed - write.

Others also wrote. Joshua, Samuel, David, Solomon and even Jezebel wrote, Esther, Jeremiah, and many more, wrote.

Jesus wrote.

Psalms 89:34 *My covenant will I not break, nor alter the thing that is gone out of my lips.*

The difference is in what they wrote. David wrote a letter to Joab, so that Uriah could be killed, and Esther wrote so that the Jews could be spared

Jesus wrote so that Mary could have life.

God wrote, so that we will never forget His character, His Godliness.

This time, in Revelation, Jesus is instructing John to write. John writes the one and only subject of Revelation - Jesus IS coming back.

It is not the subject of this book to talk about HOW Jesus would be coming back, or when Jesus is coming back.

The subject of this book is a very simple statement - Jesus is coming back.

Jesus says to John, as recorded in **Revelation 12: 6** *And he said unto me, These sayings are faithful and true: and the Lord God of the holy prophets sent his angel to shew unto his servants the things which must shortly be done.* [7] ***Behold, I come quickly:***

And in verse [12] *And,* ***behold, I come quickly***; *and my reward is with me, to give every man according as his work shall be.*

In **Revelation 3:11**, Jesus says, according to John *I am* ***coming soon***. *Hold on to what you have, so that no one*

***Psalms** 89:34 My covenant will I not break, nor alter the thing that is gone out of my lips.*

will take your crown. ¹² The one who is victorious I will make a pillar in the temple of my God. Never again will they leave it. I will write on them the name of my God and the name of the city of my God, the new Jerusalem, which is coming down out of heaven from my God; and I will also write on them my new name.

It is interesting that Jesus says to John - *These sayings are faithful and true.*

John would not have failed to believe, because John was there, all the time. John had walked with Christ, and John says in **1 John 1:1***That which was from the beginning, which we have heard, which we have seen with our eyes, which we have looked upon, and our hands have handled, of the Word of life; .... ²that eternal life, ...³ That which we have seen and heard declare we*

Matthew in **11:5** explains, *The blind receive their sight, and the lame walk, the lepers are cleansed, and the deaf hear, the dead are raised up, and the poor have the gospel preached to them.*

It was our generation that Jesus wanted to tell – that these sayings were true, that this Word, of Him and about Him, was Truth.

I am encouraged by the account written by Luke. Luke says in **Luke 4:16-22** *And he (Jesus) came to Nazareth,*

Psalms 89:34 *My covenant will I not break, nor alter the thing that is gone out of my lips.*

where he had been brought up: and, as his custom was, he went into the synagogue on the Sabbath day, and stood up for to read. [17] And there was delivered unto him the book of the prophet Esaias. And when he had opened the book, he found the place where it was written...

It is not indicated in the passage how old Jesus was when He went into the synagogue to read. This account says Jesus had done this before; He had gone into the synagogue (temple) before. This time, Jesus stood up to read.

What is interesting is that He was given the book of Isaiah to read. Was it coincidence then that Jesus read the verses that related to Him.

No, I do not believe so. There is no coincidence in the issues of God. The script Jesus read was just the right script, read at the right time by the right person.

The script went on: **Luke 4:18** *The Spirit of the Lord is upon me, because he hath anointed me to preach the gospel to the poor; he hath sent me to heal the brokenhearted, to preach deliverance to the captives, and recovering of sight to the blind, to set at liberty them that are bruised,*

This is hugely fascinating. Jesus is reading from the book of Isaiah, about the same issues that John and Mathew would talk about, confirming what Isaiah said about Christ, hundreds of years earlier.

***

Psalms 89:34 *My covenant will I not break, nor alter the thing that is gone out of my lips.*

Jesus could have read further, Jesus could have read the whole chapter:

Isaiah 61 *The Spirit of the Lord GOD is upon me; because the LORD hath anointed me to preach good tidings unto the meek; he hath sent me to bind up the brokenhearted, to proclaim liberty to the captives, and the opening of the prison to them that are bound; ² To proclaim the acceptable year of the LORD, and the day of vengeance of our God; to comfort all that mourn; ³ To appoint unto them that mourn in Zion, to give unto them beauty for ashes, the oil of joy for mourning, the garment of praise for the spirit of heaviness; that they might be called trees of righteousness, the planting of the LORD, that he might be glorified.....⁷ everlasting joy shall be unto them. ⁸ For I the LORD love judgment, I hate robbery for burnt offering; and I will direct their work in truth, and I will make an everlasting covenant with them....*

Jesus could have also stopped reading on verse 1, but He read just one more verse. This is why He had come down from heaven. He had a job to do - **Luke 4:19** reads *To preach the acceptable year of the Lord.*

Jesus was telling us, and to them that heard Him speak that day, that He was the all season Jesus, everything revolved around Him, He was the Son of the Father, the beloved Son of God.

***Psalms* 89:34** *My covenant will I not break, nor alter the thing that is gone out of my lips.*

Jesus was saying He had the message that no other could deliver, He was the ultimate sacrifice.

Jesus would tell He had come to fulfil the law, He had come to show the world the way back to God, He would preach justice and mercy, Jesus would uphold all the doctrine of Godliness.

Luke 4:20 says *And he closed the book, and he gave it again to the minister, and sat down. And the eyes of all them that were in the synagogue were fastened on him.*

I have asked, did Jesus ask for the book or was it given Him? Either way it does not matter.

The people at this place at this time, knew there was something going on, there was more to this scripture, there was more to this man called Jesus.

The Bible says in **Luke 4:21** *And he began to say unto them, This day is this scripture fulfilled in your ears. ²² And all bare him witness, and wondered at the gracious words which proceeded out of his mouth. And they said, Is not this Joseph's son?*

Yes, this was the Son of the Father, the Creator of the Universe, and the Giver of Life. He had grace written all over Him. His words were gracious.

Just so we could believe, He was also Joseph's son.

*Psalms **89:34** My covenant will I not break, nor alter the thing that is gone out of my lips.*

After Jesus had finished speaking, everyone marvelled. So what was the story about? Had He finished about the acceptable year of the Lord, or had He even talked about it, or did He even start.

The Bible indicates all He said was *This day is this scripture fulfilled in your ears.*

My thinking is, Jesus was saying that time, in that place; time had come and time would go full circle. There and then, Project Earth Rescue was just beginning. Jesus coming to earth was good, Jesus birth very good, the healing and the raising was still quite good, the death on the cross, His burial and His resurrection were coming.

The whole story, would be an awesome story, a spectacle, and it would not end there. Jesus would go back to the Father. Now we believe, Jesus is coming again.

This is where we are. Jesus says to John – write!

There is a big big story – between the going back to the Father, and the coming again. It is a story of how each of us, you and me, will overcome all, so that when Jesus comes back, He is coming back, for all, including you, including me. The story Jesus came to preach, would have come full circle.

Psalms 89:34 *My covenant will I not break, nor alter the thing that is gone out of my lips.*

Paul says to the Galatians in **Galatians 4:4** *But when the fullness of the time was come, God sent forth his Son,*

It was now up to those that heard – to believe or to reject.

Jesus is the word of God, He is the true saying.

This word converted a whole city in Samaria. It is not racist, it is fair, it is good, it is sweet, and it is powerful. The word is independent in power, in will, in thought and in counsel.

Through this Jesus, God is with us, yet out of our league. **Isaiah 66:1** says *Heaven is God's throne and the earth His footstool.*

Through Jesus, we can know, feel, and touch Godliness, on our way, back to the Father.

The Bible says in **Psalms 18:30** God's promises are true. The Psalmist says [30] *As for God, his way is perfect: the word of the LORD is tried: he is a buckler to all those that trust in him.*

And **John 9:4** says the night will come, as sure as day comes, and Paul adds, when that day comes, there will be no way of escape **1 Corinthians 10:13**.

Whatever we do, whoever we are, we need to make decisions, to choose our side.

Psalms **89:34** *My covenant will I not break, nor alter the thing that is gone out of my lips.*

Whilst we are better together, our decisions will separate us.

Small decisions, such as when and how to talk, how to walk and what to walk for, what and how to think about our situations, what and how to call our enemies, will separate us.

Jesus has the power to transform, from the inside out. **Mathew 28:18** says *And Jesus came and spake unto them, saying, All power is given unto me in heaven and in earth.*

The Bible, the word of God, is the only and final custom, the only rule, the only model of all truth and doctrine. The Bible sets the standard for everything under the sun.

2 Timothy 3:16 says *All scripture is given by inspiration of God, and is profitable for doctrine, for reproof, for correction, for instruction in righteousness:*

The Bible is its own interpreter. There is no conflict in the word of God. The challenge is with us.

Spiritual things are spiritually discerned. If we are not of the spirit, we can never understand the things of the spirit.

For good measure, Jesus says in **John 10:9** *I am the door: by me if any man enter in, he shall be saved, and shall go in and out, and find pasture.*

Psalms 89:34 *My covenant will I not break, nor alter the thing that is gone out of my lips.*

We have to do our part. God responds to our actions. You have to enter – the door is open. You have to touch the hem of His garment – Jesus wears the garment. You have to be in position, the Holy Spirit will come down. You have to do something!

This Jesus is the bread of life, the living water. He justifies, He sanctifies (makes clean). When He comes back, He will glorify.

Justice and mercy are before Him. It is not cheap mercy, there are terms and conditions. Salvation was not and is not low priced, discounted or economical. Jesus paid 100%, to redeem 100%. The redemption story has no fractions. That is why Isaiah wonders – who will believe this story.

God came down for man. He did not come on a cut-rate, or discounted. Jesus the Son of God came and paid for man's sin – pound for pound. And more. Jesus will never be the same again, after the cross – He will always have the scars left by the nails that held Him to that cross, that particular cross.

Thieves and robbers were hung on their crosses, but their crosses had no significance. Their crosses are dead wood. Jesus cross means life, it means power, it means love.

Thieves and robbers were nailed to their crosses and had scars, but their scars were not significant, the scars

Psalms 89:34 *My covenant will I not break, nor alter the thing that is gone out of my lips.*

ended when the thieves and the robbers' mortal bodies perished.

The scars Jesus had were the testimony that convinced Thomas, that Jesus was He, the scars Jesus has is the power of our salvation, the promise of eternal redemption.

Thieves and robbers bled on their crosses, but their blood had no significance. The blood dried and sank in the earth.

The blood Jesus shed is running fresh and clean. Every ounce, nothing lost. It is the blood that cleanses white as snow.

Thank God Jesus was not on the cross forever. Hours on the cross, days in the tomb and back to the Father.

Eternity beckoned, and it does even now, even this moment. There can never be anything better – for me, and by choice, for you!

My thinking is, it is good, it is very good, it is excellent to know and worship God. Going to heaven is the icing on the cake!

The difficult times in our lives will come, but Jesus says – put forward your case. We will see Jesus better, even in the fire.

Psalms 89:34 *My covenant will I not break, nor alter the thing that is gone out of my lips.*

Paul says to the **Ephesians**, in verse 4:5, *we have One God and Father of all, who is above all, and through all, and in you all. We have one faith, and one [5] One Lord, one faith, one baptism,*

These are all true sayings. We cannot talk like Christians, and act like the heathen, because Jesus, is coming back.

Chapter 3

This Same Jesus

Acts 1:4 says *And, being assembled together with them, commanded them that they should not depart from Jerusalem, but wait for the promise of the Father, which, saith he, ye have heard of me. ⁵ For John truly baptized with water; but ye shall be baptized with the Holy Ghost not many days hence. ⁶ When they therefore were come together, they asked of him, saying, Lord, wilt thou at this time restore again the kingdom to Israel?*

The disciples were promised something or someone they had never seen. They knew Jesus, but had never met the Holy Spirit. Yet they did stay in Jerusalem, waiting for someone or something they had never seen.

---

*__Psalms__ **89:34** My covenant will I not break, nor alter the thing that is gone out of my lips.*

They were just going to wait, for how long; they were never going to know.

The days were only counted after the Holy Spirit had come. To think how they knew this is what they had been waiting for is huge. They just knew, because the works of the Holy Spirit were different, they had power, huge power, and more power.

They had courage, they had faith, they believed. The disciples simply listened to the command to stay put and wait for the promise.

My question is, why would Jesus not tell them exactly when the Holy Spirit would come.

My thinking is, Jesus knew the Spirit was the prerogative of the Father. The Holy Spirit was the promise of the Father!

The disciples had been with Jesus for fourty two (42) months. The Bible is quite specific about the period Jesus was in ministry, preaching and teaching about the kingdom of heaven. Yet the same Bible would not tell when the Holy Spirit was going to come down.

How so? The time and the times belong to the Father.

Paul says the disciples asked about the purpose of His going and coming back. To the disciples, there had to be something more to the 42 months. How would Jesus preach and teach for 42 months, then just walk away – not possible!

But the thinking in the disciples' minds was not heavenly, it was earthly. The disciples thought Israel was good, but with Christ it would be best, but Jesus thought, Israel is good, but the kingdom of heaven, the kingdom of God is best.

These two (heavenly and earthly) could not compare, they are not just vastly different, in thought and practice, they are just incomparable. One is finite, the other infinite, one is heavenly, the other earthly, one is corrupt, the other incorruptible, one is eternal, one is passing, one is mortal, one is immortal.

Jesus answers the question, on the second coming. Jesus says in **Acts 1: 7**…*It is not for you to know the times or the seasons, which the Father hath put in his own power.*

True, the time is the prerogative of the Father – in everything.

Jesus reassures, in **Acts 1:8** *But ye shall receive power, after that the Holy Ghost is come upon you: and ye shall be witnesses unto me both in Jerusalem, and in all Judaea, and in Samaria, and unto the uttermost part of the earth.*

The immediate question would be, witnesses to what? I want to believe, this was the most loaded assignment ever given to the disciples, and all who would believe.

Be the witnesses.

Psalms 89:34 *My covenant will I not break, nor alter the thing that is gone out of my lips.*

The how would not be answered. The question was never verbalized anyway. It was a battle of and in the mind.

The Bible says in **Acts 1** [9] *And when he had spoken these things, while they beheld, he was taken up; and a cloud received him out of their sight.*

This is Wow, Really? He is Gone! We have an assignment – Witnesses. How did the disciples walk back? Heads raised high or shoulders slumped? I believe they believed, this Jesus, was coming back. They would walk, preach, teach, shout for joy and sing His praise, heads raised high.

There was an end game, and the disciples were going to be collaborators, co-conspirators, the disciples were going to give the evidence, that yes, this same Jesus, the one who walked this earth, the one who taught, the one who healed, the one who sympathized, this same Jesus, went to heaven.

But there was something more:

The Bible says in **Acts 1:10** *And while they looked steadfastly toward heaven as he went up, behold, two men stood by them in white apparel;* [11] *Which also said, Ye men of Galilee, why stand ye gazing up into heaven? **this same Jesus,** which is taken up from you into heaven, shall so come in like manner as ye have seen him go into heaven.*

How long did they gaze into the skies, did they cry, did they pray. What did the disciples do? How long did they stay transfixed where they had stood when Jesus was taken up? Their loving Jesus, compassionate Jesus, powerful Jesus.

Their healing Jesus, their friend, their mentor, and their counsellor.

Could they afford to go home – to what and for what? Jesus was gone. Taken into the heavens.

Some remembered the men who spoke – they had seen men like this at the tomb of Jesus.

Some remembered the voices of the men who spoke – yes, at the tomb they were there. They had reassured, Jesus has risen. That was true, so very true. They had looked at the scars, and they knew it was Jesus, they had heard His voice, and yes it was their Jesus.

This time, He is gone into HEAVEN. When will they hear His voice again? Jesus, amazing Jesus.

Every one of the disciples had his or her thoughts, they all had ideas, and they had imaginations. What if, what of – they had questions?

Yes, we know, He said it, but hey is it really true?

Psalms 89:34 *My covenant will I not break, nor alter the thing that is gone out of my lips.*

The disciples were human beings, like you and me. They had been puzzled by the story of the cross. How could their Jesus end up on the cross? How could everyone (almost everyone) be so against this amazing Jesus?

One day they would understand, another they would not be so sure, another day they would be afraid.

Then the resurrection came, and this Jesus was up from the grave – alive alive alive! Jesus was alive.

Again they could talk to Him, they could feel the scars on His hands, and they could sit with Him. I am sure the disciples would not let Jesus go, or out of sight. This was Jesus, He was with them.

Then what, He is going again, out of sight? They were exposed, how and why?

Then they remembered He commanded, stay put, until the promise of the Father comes. They had to go, maybe the promise would come before we got home, may be tomorrow. They just had to wait.

Stay there – do not move and do not be moved. Jesus had said, so they did.

This instruction was loaded. How do you stay where you are when you really do not know anything? Was there logic, what was it – faith? Was it trust? Yes, it was both, and more.

They knew Jesus. He was the covenant keeper. He was in time but lived out of time. He was believable, He was the Son of God, and He was the Christ.

Then the power came.

The message Jesus had left, you are my witnesses, was profound. It was deep, thoughtful, and reflective, it was weighty, insightful and intense.

The disciples had to do their job right.

I was not there when Jesus went back to the Father. My husband and my children were not there when Jesus was taken up to heaven. My mother was not there, neither my own earthly father. My brothers and my sisters were all not there. Even my in-laws and my friends at church were not there. You also, were not there when Jesus was taken up to heaven.

But we need to know, who was this man they called Jesus? The Bible tells us. We have read about Jesus, and we have heard about Him too.

We have just heard He did go up to heaven, We have heard He did heal, He did forgive, He did teach, He did preach, He did raise His friend Lazarus too from the dead, and saved Mary from being stoned.

We have just heard He talked about His Father, and He talked about eternity.

Psalms 89:34 *My covenant will I not break, nor alter the thing that is gone out of my lips.*

We have heard Jesus talked about Isaiah, about Moses. We have heard Jesus talked about justice and judgement.

We have heard Jesus talked about Solomon, and about the temple.

We have heard He talked about God's mercy too. We have heard about Jesus.

This Jesus I trust, I believe.

I have not just heard about Jesus. I know about Jesus and I know Jesus. He is an amazing Jesus. He walks with me, He talks to and with me, He shelters me, He gives me clothes to wear, He gives me food, He fights my battles, He protects me, I leave home with Jesus, I go places with Jesus. He is my world, He is everything to me. He loves me and I love Him so.

How do I know He is Jesus – because His works are not mistakable, He has healed me, He protects me, He has clothed me, He has and is there for me. Amazing Jesus. He has given me everything, for life and Godliness.

This Jesus is my counsellor, my hope, my strength; He is my refuge, my strong tower. He is my peace, my courage, my confidence.

This Jesus has forgiven me, and continues to forgive me, this Jesus answers my prayer. This Jesus is my friend.

But – I want more – I want to see His face; I want to feel the scars in His hands, because this Jesus, died for me. It is so very personal.

Chapter 4

Battle Of The Mind

The disciples knew the assignment, but where and how would they start?

In **Leviticus 18:3-4** Moses is passing on a message. The message, to us, seems vague, but those that heard it knew exactly what that message meant.

The Bible says in this verse, *³ After **the doings of the land of Egypt,** wherein ye dwelt, **shall ye not do: and after the doings of the land of Canaan,** whither I bring you, **shall ye not do:** neither shall ye walk in their ordinances. ⁴ Ye shall do my judgments, and keep mine ordinances, to walk therein: I am the LORD your God.*

This verse is separating the children of Israel from where they came from and where they were going. It is creating a peculiar people. They were to live in Canaan but never like the Canaanites.

Egypt they had left, so Egypt could never be part of their life – how could it? They had left Egypt and its gods, Egypt and all that Egypt could possibly mean, was behind them.

But still God had to remind them – just in case they would have desired to go back, not physically, but emotionally, mentally, socially and even spiritually. God could not live it to chance. These people Moses led were a stiff-necked people. They were a stubborn headstrong people.

The message was the same Jesus preached. But how could they be different, how could they not be like the Canaanites when it was God who was taking them there. What was the big story?

I want to believe that this would be the verse that confirms Paul's message to the Corinthians, that the word of God is "crazy stuff" to those that do not believe it.

Paul says in **1 Corinthians 1:18** *For the preaching of the cross is to them that perish foolishness; but unto us which are saved it is the power of God.*

Psalms 89:34 *My covenant will I not break, nor alter the thing that is gone out of my lips.*

The mind has a challenge – what doings shall we not do, either end of the rope, is forbidden territory, forbidden moments, forbidden times and situations.

What doings?

Paul assures us in **Philippians 2:13** when he says in verse *[13] For it is God which worketh in you both to will and to do of his good pleasure.*

Believing is a battle of the mind.

Believing God is not an academic exercise. It is not a speculative kind of investment. It is not hypothetical, or abstract. It is faith. It is confidence, trust, reliance, conviction, it is assurance, and it is devotion.

Believing the word of God is the essence of life. The Bible says in **Psalm 19:7** *The law of the LORD is perfect, converting the soul: the testimony of the LORD is sure, making wise the simple.*

When Jesus told the disciples that they were witnesses, He promised power. Power from God.

The alphabet of the Holy Spirit was not English or Japanese or Chinese. It was just awesome power, from the Father. When God speaks, everyone can hear, whether or not they want to listen, take note or pay attention.

God would not speak any earthly language; God speaks purity, righteousness, obedience. When God speaks, there is awesome power. Your life, my life, is evidence of the power of His presence.

God speaks His law and the testimony of Jesus. God speaks justice and mercy, God speaks humility. God speaks Godliness.

God knew just how tough it was going to be for the disciples. Jesus was up in heaven, beholding the children of man. The scribes and the Pharisees were still there, watching what and how the disciples were going to be and to do. So Jesus had to promise the promise of the Father.

When the Holy Spirit came down, the disciples were reassured. They were so sure Jesus was with the Father. Jesus was the real deal. Why so?

When Jesus told the disciples about the Holy Spirit, Jesus had not gone up to heaven. Jesus knew God had promised. When was that, when did God promise Jesus?

Was it in Gethsemane, was it when Jesus got baptized in the Jordan, was it when He went alone to pray, was it before He was born in the manger?

This just meant Jesus knew the way heaven worked and works. When and how had Jesus been told by His Father that the Holy Spirit would come? Jesus was the Son of the Father, Jesus and His Father were one.

Psalms 89:34 *My covenant will I not break, nor alter the thing that is gone out of my lips.*

Jesus says in **John 10:30** *I and my Father are one.*

Jesus was so sure – go and wait in Jerusalem, for the promise of the Father!

Jesus cares. He gives us something to work with. He gave us the Holy Spirit. Witnesses have evidence, witnesses are compelling, because they were there, they heard and they saw.

Jesus gives power to discern, power to do, power to plan, power to work, power to pray.

The instruction came with awesome power. It was control power, influence, authority, supremacy, power to rule, to command, it was clout, it was muscle.

This kind of power, the disciples knew very well. Jesus had that kind of power. He says in **Matthew 28:18-20** *And Jesus came and spake unto them, saying, All power is given unto me in heaven and in earth. ¹⁹ Go ye therefore, and teach all nations, baptizing them in the name of the Father, and of the Son, and of the Holy Ghost: ²⁰ Teaching them to observe all things whatsoever I have commanded you: and, lo, I am with you always, even unto the end of the world.*

The disciples also knew – the Romans had power. The Romans were in charge when Jesus was taken up. But with all that power, the Caesars could not stop the resurrection, they could not stop the ascension, they could not stop the Holy Spirit coming down.

The power of heaven came. It came in tongues of fire. It was power that would change lives.

It was power that gave a mind that could separate Egypt from Canaan, and it was power that could separate those that lived in Canaan from those that came into Canaan.

It was clarity power, it was compassion power.

This power took away the confusion, the presumptions; it is power that focuses, which builds, and it is power that overcomes.

It is power that takes away the doubt, the infirmities, it is power that separates.

When Moses was instructed, Israel would and had to be different, from Egypt and the Egyptians, and also different from Canaan and the Canaanites;

This would have been thoroughly confusing, without this kind of power, the power Jesus promised.

It was the promise of the Father; The Creator of the Universe, the Giver of Life, the Former of All Things.

We know what happened in Egypt – it was gross. Everything for us was bad. For the Egyptians it was home, they had Pharaoh, they had everything, but hey, for us, even in Goshen, when Joseph had died, it was bad. That was Egypt, and Israel longed for something better.

Psalms 89:34 *My covenant will I not break, nor alter the thing that is gone out of my lips.*

But what of Canaan? Moses could have reasoned and questioned. We are enroute there and yet we ought to be different. How so, is it ever possible?

Yes it was possible. To Canaan they were going, a land filled with milk and honey. Yes, filled with milk and honey. It was not about the milk, or the honey, it was about what the Canaanites believed.

In Egypt milk was also there, and so was the honey. God could have left the children of Israel there, and provided the milk and the honey there. But Egypt was not Canaan. Canaan was different; it was *filled* with milk and honey. There was no space for anything different, but hey, the gods of the Canaanites were also there, as much as Pharaoh was in Egypt.

The instructions were, even when the milk and the honey fills up your dwelling place, the gods of that place are not for you.

This was where the witnessing would start.

Egypt was really bad, but even in Israel among the chosen, the Jews; the thinking would also be bad. The children of Israel had been contaminated by the doings of Canaan. The disciples needed to know, you witness what you saw, what you heard, what you touched.

The disciples had to bring people back to the only true God, the Creator of the Universe, the Giver of Life, to the Former of All things.

There would be no room for confusion. There needed to be clarity of purpose, clarity in life.

It was a battle of the mind – the laws, the testimonies and the grace.

Jesus needed faithful witnesses. A true witness needed to have been there. They had to be correct, true, authentic, and accurate, they had to be exact.

It was going to be easy and it was easy for the disciples to say – yes, we were there when Jesus was taken up with the clouds; yes we were there when He healed the sick, or raised the dead, or fed the five thousand, and the four thousand.

That was the easiest part of the witnessing. They were there.

How would they then preach that Jesus was coming back?

John 16:7 says *Nevertheless I tell you the truth; It is expedient for you that I go away: for if I go not away, the Comforter will not come unto you; but if I depart, I will send him unto you.*

Jesus had promised, and the disciples knew they had to wait. When the Holy Spirit came, they knew their promise, what Jesus promised, the promise of the Father, had come.

Psalms **89:34** *My covenant will I not break, nor alter the thing that is gone out of my lips.*

The disciples were very clear: Jesus would not have come so that for fourty two months He would just heal and feed. No, there had to be something better, something more.

It was about and of the kingdom of God. That was more.

Chapter 5

The Quake, The Smoke & The Cloud

God is all knowing. He is gracious; He is the most merciful Father. God cares. He knows our mind is too small to believe the word of God. Too small to comprehend the invisible God.

So God gives us something to work with, something we understand, something we can relate, something we know.

It is not that man do not want God, no, man does not know God. To know God is to love Him, for God is love.

Psalms **89:34** *My covenant will I not break, nor alter the thing that is gone out of my lips.*

The children of Israel had crossed the red sea, they had been pulled out of Pharaoh's hand, they had seen the fire by night and the cloud by day, that led them out of Egypt.

These children of Israel had seen the power of God, but they had not seen God. In their mind the power was separate from the Owner of that power. So God decides to show up, in an earthquake, in the smoke and in the cloud.

God knew these children of Jacob could not see God and live. God and disobedience are not friends. But God has loved, before, He will love again, and He loves throughout eternity.

God tells Moses in **Exodus 19:9** *And the LORD said unto Moses, Lo, I come unto thee in a thick cloud, that the people may hear when I speak with thee, and believe thee forever. And Moses told the words of the people unto the LORD.*

God came down in a thick cloud so that the children of Israel could behold Him. God had to make a plan, and He did.

In **Exodus 19:4-6** the Lord tells Moses to tell the people, *[4] Ye have seen what I did unto the Egyptians, and how I bare you on eagles' wings, and brought you unto myself. [5] Now therefore, if ye will obey my voice indeed, and keep my covenant, then ye shall be a peculiar treasure unto me above all people: for all the earth is mine: [6] And* *ye shall be unto me a kingdom of priests, and an holy nation.*

This is God, reminding, gently persuading for obedience. This is God promising. This is God wanting His children to obey Him, to see Him as their God.

God is reminding them of **Exodus 13:21,** which says *And the LORD went before them by day in a pillar of a cloud, to lead them the way; and by night in a pillar of fire, to give them light; to go by day and night:*

Hundreds of years later, Nehemiah would pray *Yet thou in thy manifold mercies forsookest them not in the wilderness: the pillar of the cloud departed not from them by day, to lead them in the way; neither the pillar of fire by night, to shew them light, and the way wherein they should go.* **Nehemiah 9:19**

Nehemiah would pray more *Moreover thou leddest them in the day by a cloudy pillar; and in the night by a pillar of fire, to give them light in the way wherein they should go.* **Nehemiah 9:12**

The Lord is that good. He gives us something to work with. Just so we may believe, just so we may choose Him as our God.

God gives us real life experiences to work with. If we may just remember how He has led us through this great

---

Psalms 89:34 *My covenant will I not break, nor alter the thing that is gone out of my lips.*

wilderness. This life can be dry and intimidating. God delivers, goes before us, just so we can say – The Lord God is our God.

In **Deuteronomy 1:33**, Moses says to the children of Israel, it is God *[33] Who went in the way before you, to search you out a place to pitch your tents in, in fire by night, to shew you by what way ye should go, and in a cloud by day.*

This is huge. Moses is explaining to people who actually saw these things. It was not hearsay, they were there, yet they would not really obey God.

Where we camp is where we seat. Where we camp is very important. We camp with people of like mind. We camp where our needs are met.

Moses is saying God is particular. He cares. He wants to authorize where and how we camp, in whose territory, and how long we can stay there.

Moses says God went before them to search for a place where they could pitch their tents.

Where, is directional. It defines the co-ordinates of our lives. Where we camp, where we pitch our tents, defines who we are. God is concerned about who we are and who we become.

The wilderness is full, very full of scorpions, stones and snakes. These people would not have survived the desert, if the Lord had not gone before them.

Yet they would be so quick, at the slightest prick, to turn away from God.

Moses would say to the children of Israel, in **Deuteronomy 2:7** *For the LORD thy God hath blessed thee in all the works of thy hand: he knoweth thy walking through this great wilderness: these forty years the LORD thy God hath been with thee; thou hast lacked nothing.*

The children of Israel just forgot, or is it that they just did not care?

How could they not care? How could they not remember the fear when they knew Pharaoh was right behind them, how could they forget so easily?

How could they not remember that particular morning? The Bible confirms in **Exodus 14:24** *And it came to pass, that in the morning watch the LORD looked unto the host of the Egyptians through the pillar of fire and of the cloud, and troubled the host of the Egyptians,*

This was the situation in the camp of Israel when the Lord decided to make contact on Mount Sinai.

Psalms 89:34 *My covenant will I not break, nor alter the thing that is gone out of my lips.*

God gave instructions to Moses in **Exodus 19:11.** God said *And be ready against the third day: for the third day the* LORD *will come down in the sight of all the people upon mount Sinai.*

The Lord is very consistent. He is an equal opportunity God. He gave to all, time to prepare to meet with God. He cares that much He wanted everyone safe from the fright, the fear and the death that followed seeing God outside repentance, outside cleanliness, outside obedience. God gave the instruction because He knew the children of Israel. They lived outside the presence of God, yet under the cloud of His presence; they lived in darkness yet covered by the fire of the Lord's light.

God says to Moses, prepare to meet me. In this particular occasion the Lord says get ready against the third day. God mentions what to expect on that third day. The Lord says to Moses, for the third day the Lord will come down in the sight of all the people upon Mount Sinai.

The Lord's coming in public view was not small. It was phenomenal. When we ask the Lord to come down and be amongst us, in Church or elsewhere. This is not and should never be small.

It is huge for the Lord to come down, so that the finite can behold the infinite. When the Lord comes down, to deal with our situations, our lives, that is huge.

Man ought to prepare against the third day – the day the Lord has decided He wants to be seen. Whatever that day shall be, it shall be our third day. We cannot see God without preparation.

Whilst man has no clear record of which particular peak, the highest mountain on the range of mountains known as the Sinai Mountains was good enough for God to show Himself to Moses. It was a good enough mount for God to show up and write His commandments.

God could have written the Ten Commandments elsewhere and brought them to Moses. God could have landed the stone tablets from heaven, right to the centre of the camp, God could have sent special courier with the commandments, but God did not.

The Bible says in **Exodus 24:12** *And the LORD said unto Moses, Come up to me into the mount, and be there: and I will give thee tables of stone, and a law, and commandments which I have written; that thou mayest teach them.*

Psalms **89:34** *My covenant will I not break, nor alter the thing that is gone out of my lips.*

It was important that God showed up, to Moses and to deliver the Ten Commandments. God would write the Ten Commandments in the presence of Moses. Moses had to see God write His laws, His character, on Mt. Sinai stone! Moses had to testify, God wrote with His finger. It was important.

Wikipedia.org. (January, 2019). *Mount Sinai 9*. [online]. Available at: https://en.wikipedia.org/wiki/Mount_Sinai 9 [Accessed February 22, 2019]

Moses would later say *And he (God) declared unto you his covenant, which he commanded you to perform, even ten commandments; and he wrote them upon two tables of stone.* **Deuteronomy 4:13**

And the LORD delivered unto me two tables of stone written with the finger of God; and on them was written according to all the words, which the LORD spake with you in the mount out of the midst of the fire in the day of the assembly. **Deuteronomy 9:10**

God decided to show Himself on that rugged terrain, on that particular route, at that particular time. It was important; it was a declaration of Godliness by God, the Creator of the Universe, the Giver of Life. Those Ten Commandments were a covenant.

An atheist would love the Ten Commandments; the Greeks would love them as much as the Jews would. All institutions love the Ten Commandments, all nations, all tongues, all people.

Not everyone would declare them publicly, not everyone would want to obey them, not everyone would seek to know the writer, the author, but everyone, in one way or the other, is inadvertently looking to the Ten Commandments.

The Atheist will say there is no God, but he unintentionally, involuntarily, accidentally and even unconsciously, looks to the Ten Commandments – for redress, for fairness, for justice.

This is the power of the Ten Commandment Covenant.

It is recorded that Mount Sinai is 2 285 meters high, and stand 332 meters above or higher than the next mountain.

Psalms 89:34 *My covenant will I not break, nor alter the thing that is gone out of my lips.*

My thinking was, why did God not give the Ten Commandments at the Red sea, soon after crossing would have been good. Or at the waters of Marah. Why would God choose a range of mountains, the peak of it, for this declaration?

My search indicates this interesting fact:

Water affects sound waves in several ways. For example, sound move several times faster through water than air, and travel longer distances. However, because the human ear was made to hear in air, water tends to muffle sounds that are otherwise clear in air. Water can also "bend" sound, sending it on a zigzag path instead of a straight line.

Johnson S., Sciencing.com (April 24, 2018)., . *How Does Water Affect Sound?* [online]. Available at: https://sciencing.com/water-affect-sound-8510076.html [January 2019]

The declaration was so important God did not want His voice muffled by the waters of the red sea, or even by the waters of Marah. God did not want His words, His instructions, going in the wrong direction.

God wanted the echo of the mountains, God wanted the stability of the mountains, and God wanted the height of Mount Sinai. God wanted to be heard, in the quake, in the fire and in the cloud.

The children of Israel had to be good enough to stand. The wind and all would be alert to the presence of God. When God speaks, the winds and the waves obey God, they give God His space and His place.

When God says peace be still, nature responds, no questions asked. Man will ask why and how, as if man really does not know. The earthquakes, the smoke and the clouds are in attention when the Lord shows up.

So the children of Israel had to prepare against that day.

The Bible says in **Exodus 19:20** *And the LORD came down upon mount Sinai, on the top of the mount: and the LORD called Moses up to the top of the mount; and Moses went up.*

In this Bible record, it seems like it was so simple for Moses to go up and down the mountain. It also seems the voice of the Lord was just a voice. The Bible says, *and the Lord spoke to Moses in a voice.*

This is God, speaking in the midst of a range of mountains, whilst on top of the high point on that range on their route.

Moses, God had made just good enough to stand. Moses was not equal to God, he was not a son, he was not an angel. Moses was like you, he was like me, but Moses was an obedient servant. If and when he talked with God, the agenda was the same, so they could walk, they could talk, they could plan, they could see, they could just "flock" together.

Psalms 89:34 *My covenant will I not break, nor alter the thing that is gone out of my lips.*

God will meet with us on our route. Whatever route that is. When we do, we will either run away from God, or we will stand and commune with God.

Touregypt.net. (1996-2019). *Mount Sinai (and the peak of Mount Musa or Mousa).* [online].
Available at:

http://www.touregypt.net/featurestories/mountsinai.htm [Accessed February 22, 2019]

This picture does not give an impression that getting to the top of the mount was easy. It was a challenge.

And the voice calling from that mountain must have produced an awesome echo.

This was God calling. He chooses the time and the place, but He does show up.

In **Exodus 19** the Bible says *³ And Moses went up unto God, and the LORD called unto him out of the mountain, saying, Thus shalt thou say to the house of Jacob, and tell the children of Israel; ⁴ Ye have seen what I did unto the Egyptians, and how I bare you on eagles' wings, and brought you unto myself. ⁵ Now therefore, if ye will obey my voice indeed, and keep my covenant, then ye shall be a peculiar treasure unto me above all people: for all the earth is mine:*

The Lord will always show Himself, the route that we walk He has mapped out, He knows the hills and the mountains on this route, and He knows exactly when to show up.

God starts by stating how He took the children of Israel out of Egypt – on eagle's wings! God knew what He was doing in Egypt; He was going to let them know He was in charge, ninety days later.

Ninety days was very long in the desert. That is why when Moses went up fourty days on Mount Sinai the children of Israel just decided, enough, Egypt was better.

No, it was not and would never have been better, but the mind does play tricks on us. The mind can choose what it remembers; the mind can also choose to weigh, balance out and make logic out of what it remembers.

Psalms 89:34 *My covenant will I not break, nor alter the thing that is gone out of my lips.*

The important can be made of no significance, and the not important can be made important.

What is clear is, how we remember is consequential. That is why God had to mention, *note how I bare you on eagle's wings.*

The ninety days in the desert, these people had to remember, it was on eagle's wings that we came out of Egypt. Pharaoh was powerful; it just needed the awesome power of God to make a way out of Egypt. Even though the route was the long way home, the long way to a promise, was just better!

It did not and does not matter how long the journey is, because God's presence goes with us, and before us.

The Bible says in **Exodus 19:18** *And mount Sinai was altogether on a smoke, because the LORD descended upon it in fire: and the smoke thereof ascended as the smoke of a furnace, and the whole mount quaked greatly.*

This text says the whole mount was on fire. The Lord filled up the whole place. God did not instruct the mountain to quake; the mountain quaked on its own. How could it not? The Master had come down. The master of the wind and the maker of the rain had taken His place!

The mountains knew, this God had the universe in the palms of His hands.

The Bible says in **Micah 1:4** *The mountains melt beneath Him and the valleys split apart*, and

Nahum 1:5 says *the mountains quake before him and hills melt away. The earth trembles at His presence, the world and all who live in it.*

When Moses went down to give the law to the children of Israel, the Bible does not tell us if God left the mountain. God had no need to go anywhere. God is Omni-present. He is everywhere, in time and in place.

The Lord is all-knowing. The Lord knew Moses was going to break the two tables of stone. God allowed Moses to go through the emotions, the hurt and sometimes even the doubt, but Moses knew one thing – he could always go back to God. Moses also knew he could not be deliberate in disregarding the principles, or God's covenant, but if he erred, Moses knew God would forgive.

We read in chapter 34, that God instructs Moses to hew two tablets of stone like the first which Moses had broken.

The Bible says in **Exodus 34** *And the LORD said unto Moses, Hew thee two tables of stone like unto the first: and I will write upon these tables the words that were in the first tables, which thou brakest.*

Psalms 89:34 *My covenant will I not break, nor alter the thing that is gone out of my lips.*

God is saying to Moses, sort out what you broke. God is saying, I forgive you Moses, but sort out what you broke!

God knew what Moses was going to face when Moses came down the mountain, but God did not stop writing the two tables of stone. He did. When Moses broke the stones, God did not shout at Moses, God said, give me the same that I gave you.

This is an awesome God. My thinking is, God was testing Moses. It was not even about the children of Israel, it was about Moses.

God could have forewarned Moses, God could have postponed giving the law to Moses, God could have preserved the two tables of stone, God could have stopped the children of Israel from building the calf, but God did not.

Neither did Moses complain to God asking why God did not do all and all and all.

Moses said, you know Lord, these people do not listen – they are a stiff necked people.

And God agreed. That is exactly the word God used to describe the children of Israel.

So God knows, He is just testing testing! When God is done testing, we are better than we ever thought we could be. God is the refiner.

Malachi 3:3 would say *And he shall sit as a refiner and purifier of silver: and he shall purify the sons of Levi, and purge them as gold and silver, that they may offer unto the LORD an offering in righteousness.*

In **Exodus 34:2**, the Lord says to Moses *And be ready in the morning, and come up in the morning unto mount Sinai, and present thyself there to me in the top of the mount.* **Exodus 34**

I can only imagine what Moses felt. Despondent? Possibly. But God says come up again, in the morning.

The mountain was not an easy mount, but Moses would go up and down for the children of Israel and their God.

God did not even make it easier for Moses; God still wanted Moses to come to the top of the mountain. There, is where God wanted Moses to present himself.

As this writer would say in the book The Lord Our Habitation, Moses was power shovelling for God. Moses had just passed the test. Moses had walked with God, but Moses now knew God.

When Moses went up, then God descended. The Bible says [5] *And the LORD descended in the cloud, and stood with him there, and proclaimed the name of the LORD.* **Exodus 34.**

***Psalms* 89:34** *My covenant will I not break, nor alter the thing that is gone out of my lips.*

This is fascinating. Arguably, God is the one who is proclaiming the name of the Lord. Is that true?

The Bible says ⁶ *And the LORD passed by before him, and proclaimed, The LORD, The LORD God, merciful and gracious, longsuffering, and abundant in goodness and truth, ⁷ Keeping mercy for thousands, forgiving iniquity and transgression and sin, and that will by no means clear the guilty; visiting the iniquity of the fathers upon the children, and upon the children's children, unto the third and to the fourth generation. ⁸ And Moses made haste, and bowed his head toward the earth, and worshipped.* **Exodus 34**

This reads like it. That God proclaimed who He was to Moses, and Moses bowed down and worshipped. The Bible records that Moses ⁹ ···· *said, If now I have found grace in thy sight, O LORD, let my LORD, I pray thee, go among us; for it is a stiff-necked people; and pardon our iniquity and our sin, and take us for thine inheritance.* **Exodus 34**

Yes, God was merciful and Moses was witness. How could God be so patient, so powerful yet so gentle?

God says to Moses in verse 10 *Behold, I make a covenant: before all thy people I will do marvels, such as have not been done in all the earth, nor in any nation: and all the people among which thou art shall see the work of the LORD: for it is a terrible thing that I will do with thee.* **Exodus 34**

What was that which was going to be so terrible? And how were the tribes of Israel to be protected – one way!

Exodus 34:11says *Observe thou that which I command thee this day: behold, I drive out before thee the Amorite, and the Canaanite, and the Hittite, and the Perizzite, and the Hivite, and the Jebusite.*

God wanted the children of Israel to see what and how God was going to drive out the Canaanites. The children of Israel were not going to do this particular work, driving out people. God was going to. The Lord goes on to say;

¹² Take heed to thyself, lest thou make a covenant with the inhabitants of the land whither thou goest, lest it be for a snare in the midst of thee:

The children of Israel were going to listen, to note, and to take heed. God was going to deal with the people, and the children of Israel were going to, as the Bible says *¹³ .... destroy their altars, break their images, and cut down their groves*: **Exodus 34**

God was very protective. He knew the children of Israel would not be able to drive out their enemies, but they would be able to clear what their enemies left. God also wanted the children of Israel to choose their God. They had to destroy the gods of the Canaanites, in order to serve God.

Psalms 89:34 *My covenant will I not break, nor alter the thing that is gone out of my lips.*

In verse 14 God says [14] *For thou shalt worship no other god: for the LORD, whose name is Jealous, is a jealous God:* **Exodus 34**

God was saying to the children of Israel – I resent other gods, because there is just no other God. Your gods would be figments of your imagination. God is saying you cannot invent God, you cannot hallucinate about God, you cannot fabricate God, and there is just no other God.

God was saying you have seen what I do and how I do it, you have seen how much I care, so how, how can you even think…!

God is God. Either you are His or you are not. God has His standards. He will not accept compromise, yet He will accept those that return to Him, in whatever state.

The Bible goes on to say [15] *Lest thou make a covenant with the inhabitants of the land, and they go a whoring after their gods, and do sacrifice unto their gods, and one call thee, and thou eat of his sacrifice;* **Exodus 34**

The verse above says no contact, whatever you do, no contact because they may call you and you will, inadvertently, eat their sacrifice. Wow. God sure is a jealous God. God just does not want.

If you are called by the name of the Lord, you also just cannot!

It is not in vain that we worship God. God says in verse 24 *For I will cast out the nations before thee, and enlarge thy borders: neither shall any man desire thy land, when thou shalt go up to appear before the LORD thy God thrice in the year.* **Exodus 34.**

Arguably, the Bible is saying, if God does not stand guard over your land, someone may desire it and will want to take it away from you when you are out worshipping Him.

So God is making sure your inheritance will not be challenged. God will drive away everyone who may just want to take what is yours.

God cares that much. He stands guard over what He has given us. What a caring God.

[27] *And the LORD said unto Moses, Write thou these words: for after the tenor of these words I have made a covenant with thee and with Israel.* **Exodus 34.**

The Lord says to Moses; write these words, because this is what I will do. This is the basis of our covenant. [28] *And he (Moses) was there with the LORD forty days and forty nights; he did neither eat bread, nor drink water. And he wrote upon the tables the words of the covenant, the Ten Commandments.* **Exodus 34.**

This time Moses was up the mountain fourty days and fourty nights. Wow!

Psalms **89:34** *My covenant will I not break, nor alter the thing that is gone out of my lips.*

So what were the mountains doing for fourty days, and was the cloud still there? The Bible does not say, but what we know is, the Lord was in the quake, in the smoke and in the cloud, on Mount Sinai.

The reason; God was declaring, He was stating the facts, the *modus operandi* of life. God was making a promise. God's presence had to be seen, to be felt. God is God.

So was He, on Mount Calvary.

The crowds of Mathew 27 shouted that Jesus be crucified. Not only that, they shouted that the blood of Jesus be upon them and their children.

How so right they were. It is the blood of Jesus that we plead on our lives and that of our children. It is the blood of Jesus that gives us hope; it is the blood of Jesus that gives us a future. It is the blood of Jesus that sets free, that delivers, and that washes whiter than snow.

Barabbas would not have helped. Barabbas would have died without a chance to life eternal. Even Barabbas, because Jesus died for all, would have a chance to heaven's gates, to heaven's everything.

Barabbas also needed Jesus to die for him. Yes the crowd was right. Barabbas had to be set free, not by the crowd, but because Jesus had just taken his place.

The Bible says in **Mathew 27:25** *Then answered all the people, and said, His blood be on us, and on our children.*

The governor Pilate asked just the right question. The Bible says in **Mathew 27:23** *And the governor said, Why, what evil hath he done? But they cried out the more, saying, Let him be crucified.*

It was all so correct. Jesus had done nothing evil. That is the very reason why only Him, Jesus, could be crucified, for you and for me. Jesus was qualified to take my place, according to the dictates of God. Only one blameless could redeem. Now I live, in every aspect of existence, I have life, because Jesus took my place.

Just like on Sinai, God the Father knew the lost that Moses had left behind, could not do right. They were a stiff necked people. So were the crowds of Mathew 27. But the Lord did not spare Moses the experience, or Jesus the moment of agony, because these two, knew the price of sacrifice – the kingdom of God.

The Bible says in **Mathew 27:51** *And, behold, the veil of the temple was rent in twain from the top to the bottom; and the earth did quake, and the rocks rent; [52] And the graves were opened; and many bodies of the saints which slept arose,........[54] Now when the centurion, and they that were with him, watching Jesus, saw the earthquake, and those things that were done, they feared greatly, saying, Truly this was the Son of God.*

Psalms 89:34 *My covenant will I not break, nor alter the thing that is gone out of my lips.*

Yes He was, yes He is. Yes Jesus and His Father are one. The rocks and the mountains knew it, and they could not keep silent. They had to say something. What the mountains and the rocks said, the centurion and those around him heard; Jesus was and is the Son of God.

Even the sun could not shine. The Lord was on the cross. For three good hours the sun could not share its light. The sun was speaking for humanity. This is the Christ, the Son of God, the Creator of the Universe, the Giver of Life.

The crowd of Mathew 27 was a witness. It was a thick cloud of witnesses. These would tell that the Lord came down on Mount Calvary. The Father came down for the Son.

Jesus was right, where man could not speak, the rocks could, and on mount Calvary they did, the rocks spoke.

How could man not know?

━━━ *Chapter 6* ━━━

Fully Covered

The word of God is our assurance, and the blood of Jesus is our insurance.

The word of God declares the Excellency of God, it promises everlasting life. The blood of Jesus manifests, makes real, demonstrates, reveals and establishes that truth, the truth of the word of God.

The blood of Jesus makes possible which was beyond us – it makes real the fact that human beings, who fell so short of the glory of God, who would die if they saw God, would really see God, someday, sometime, and not die.

Psalms 89:34 *My covenant will I not break, nor alter the thing that is gone out of my lips.*

The blood of Jesus covers us, from a multitude of sin, it protects us from the shame and nakedness that sin brings, it exonerates, and it indemnifies us from the punishment of disobedience – it is our insurance ONLY when we return to God.

David says in **Psalm 32:1** *Blessed is he whose transgression is forgiven, whose sin is covered.*

And Paul would say in **Romans 4:6-8** *Even as David also describeth the blessedness of the man, unto whom God imputeth righteousness without works,* **[7] Saying, Blessed are they whose iniquities are forgiven, and whose sins are covered.**

Paul is acknowledging what David said, hundreds of years earlier. Both had a story to tell. Both knew the freedom that forgiveness and being forgiven mean.

David and Paul just wanted one thing – to be forgiven. Jesus was there, in the span of time, to forgive both. Jesus knows everything that happens under the sun, in the whole universe, with its galaxies and open skies.

Jesus knows what goes on, beneath the earth, in the depths of the seas and in the heart of man.

God knows our thoughts, God reads our minds, and God knows everything.

Everything about man on earth, what man is and what man thinks, outside God, is not good. It is impure. The

Bible says the mind and heart of man was and is continuously thinking evil. This is why God sent His Son, for our redemption.

Against the day of the Lord, this kind of thinking does not stand. Someone had to bridge the gap; someone had to stand in the breach. Only Jesus could, He was the promise of the Father, as Isaiah would say.

The heavens opened for Jesus, and the Holy Spirit of the Lord most High descended on Jesus. This was evidence that the Father above, the Holy Spirit and Jesus, were in cohorts, they were partners, and they were associates. In fact, their bond was and is much bigger – they are one. They cared and care about what goes on under the sun, on the earth.

The Bible in **Mark 1:10** says *And straightway coming up out of the water, he saw the heavens opened, and the Spirit like a dove descending upon him:*

This is huge. The whole heavens opened. They were in salute. The Son of the Father was going for baptism. Really?

The Co-Creator was on a mission. Mission was not impossible, it was mission Fourty Two Months! Wow. Yes, really!

Psalms 89:34 *My covenant will I not break, nor alter the thing that is gone out of my lips.*

The Bible says in **John 1:32,** *And John bare record, saying, I saw the Spirit descending from heaven like a dove, and it abode upon him.*

This was the Lord showing us that for man, He had come down. How could heaven open so the Spirit of the Lord, the "size" of a dove, could come down? No, it was not that small, the earth was just fully covered by the grace of God. The "dove" was what we could see, what we could relate. God was giving us something to work with.

It was not going to matter what colour you were and are, it would not matter where in the world you stood; the earth was fully covered, by grace, by love, by power!

This was not the first time the Lord, and the Spirit of the Lord, would come down, and neither was it going to be the last.

In the Garden of Eden the Lord used to come down, in the cool of the evening, to commune with man.

The Bible says in **Genesis 3: 8** *And they heard the voice of the LORD God walking in the garden in the cool of the day: and Adam and his wife hid themselves from the presence of the LORD God amongst the trees of the garden. ⁹ And the LORD God called unto Adam, and said unto him, Where art thou? ¹⁰ And he said, I heard thy voice in the garden, and I was afraid, because I was naked; and I hid myself. ¹¹ And he said, Who told thee that thou wast naked? Hast thou eaten of the tree, whereof I commanded thee that thou shouldest not eat?*

It is nakedness that we are all running away from. We even think we can hide our nakedness from God.

God visited Adam and Eve, in their naked hour, so that Adam and Eve would know no one can run away from God and truly hide.

As much as some will believe there is no God, the same would believe, if per adventure He was there, they believe they can cover themselves. No, no one can. Only God covers. When He does, we are fully and completely covered.

The shame is gone, the nakedness is gone.

Paul says in **Hebrews 4:12** *For the word of God is quick, and powerful, and sharper than any twoedged sword, piercing even to the dividing asunder of soul and spirit, and of the joints and marrow, and is a discerner of the thoughts and intents of the heart. [13] Neither is there any creature that is not manifest in his sight: but all things are naked and opened unto the eyes of him with whom we have to do.*

The word of the Lord can uncover you, and the blood of Jesus covers up. The word of the Lord makes you see your nakedness, and the same word is so effective in letting you know when and how you can get covered.

It is really a two edged sword, so so powerful, piercing even to the dividing asunder of soul and spirit.

Psalms 89:34 *My covenant will I not break, nor alter the thing that is gone out of my lips.*

How powerful. So powerful yet so smooth. When it has finished with you there are no rough edges. It is all so there. Nothing missing, nothing lost. This is the word of God and the power of His presence in our lives.

The Bible says in *Exodus 33:14 **And he said, My presence shall go with thee, and I will give thee rest.***

Our biggest fear should be – to live outside the presence of God.

Adam and Eve hid themselves from the presence of the Lord, but the Lord is everywhere.

The Bible says Adam and Eve heard the voice of the Lord, and the Lord was walking in the garden.

The question is, was God "singing" so they could hear His voice, was He talking, was the Trinity discussing Adam and Eve? Because Adam says we heard the voice. Or did Adam and Eve just remember what God had said. God had spoken, God had given the instructions, so what nature of a voice did Adam and Eve hear?

The evening was a good time to commune with the Lord. The sun was setting. Is it then that Adam and Eve remembered, when the noise around them was gone and it was quieter, when they had "clarity" of what and on what they had done?

When Adam and Eve had sinned against God, they still heard the voice of the Lord. When the Lord speaks, it does not matter where you are or who you are, you will hear His voice. We still have a choice, to accept or reject.

The Bible says God asked them where they were and what had happened. Really, God asking man what had happened?

This is mercy mercy mercy. God was asking man to explain himself, to put forward his case.

The word of the Lord says in Hebrews, everything is open and naked before Him. Adam and Eve had lost the glory of the Lord. The glory of the Lord just wound off their beings. They were suddenly exposed.

That is what sin does. It exposes. God's presence covers.

The Lord let Adam and Eve hear His voice well before He called them. This is God. He did not want to take these naked people by surprise; He was gentle, like He did not know. Adam and Eve got an opportunity to cover themselves, but their cover was not enough, they still needed God Himself to cover them.

The gold of the river Pishon could not cover Adam and Eve, the multitude of trees and shrubs could not cover them, neither the herds of elephants, buffalos and hippos. The flowers could not give their nakedness any beauty, God had to come down to cover His own – in

Psalms 89:34 *My covenant will I not break, nor alter the thing that is gone out of my lips.*

the cool of the evening, when Adam and Eve could hear God more.

Men have a tendency to hear God or want to listen to God more when they are naked. When all is well, God is, well, god.

Adam and Eve must have done what they did early in the day, because they needed time to think of how to cover themselves. They then had to sew the leaves together, look for the big and strong. Unfortunately, their cover was just leaves – though big and strong, but they were just leaves!

God will give us time. Time enough to sew our own leaves. Time enough to wear them. He will give us time so the leaves can dry out and then we will listen when He speaks. God is patient.

The enemy's plan and purpose is to expose us, and without the mercies of God we are exposed, it does not matter what we do and how we do it. We just need the Lord Himself to cover us.

Jesus came, so that we are fully and completely covered from the shame that nakedness brings.

God comes to deliver. In **2 Samuel 22:10** the Bible says *He bowed the heavens also, and came down; and darkness was under his feet.*

This was David talking, praising God for the deliverance that David had seen.

Saul pursued David not to make friends or to talk, Saul pursued David to destroy David and all that David stood for. What Saul never knew was God was the reason behind David. David had truly been afraid, *sore* afraid. David would say in

2 Samuel 22:4 *I will call on the LORD, who is worthy to be praised: so shall I be saved from mine enemies. [5] When the waves of death compassed me, the floods of ungodly men made me afraid; [6] The sorrows of hell compassed me about; the snares of death prevented me; [7] In my distress I called upon the LORD, and cried to my God: and he did hear my voice out of his temple, and my cry did enter into his ears. [8] Then the earth shook and trembled; the foundations of heaven moved and shook,*

Yes, the Lord will deliver, out of all our distress. David had already been anointed. David had already been covered.

The cover we may not feel, or touch it, or smell it, but it is there. Saul did not see it either, and David, at times, he was not sure, but it was there. After the event, when peace prevailed, David would praise the Lord.

This is the Lord, when He came down at Sinai the earth quaked, when He came down for David, in David's life, everything shook.

Psalms 89:34 *My covenant will I not break, nor alter the thing that is gone out of my lips.*

Nothing remains the same, when the Lord comes down. We will be witnesses, faithful witnesses, that the Lord came down, for us.

When the Lord comes down to deliver, the one that got delivered will know that the foundations, of whatever, shook for him or her.

Other people may never know, but those that heard the voice, those that saw, those that touched, will know and say, the Lord came down for me.

This is what David says in **Psalm 18:9** *He bowed the heavens also, and came down: and darkness was under his feet.*

David was so confident he could pray, as he did in **Psalm 144:5** *Bow thy heavens, O LORD, and come down: touch the mountains, and they shall smoke.*

The Lord had done it before for David; God had given David something to work with. When things got bad in chapter 144, David would pray, bow thy heavens Oh Lord, and come down.

David had that confidence, that when the Lord does come down, even the mountains of our lives will smoke!

These mountain things in our lives are really quite a challenge. They instil fear, they are huge in our eyes, and they make us doubt God. Even God's power shovels, like Isaiah, would pray;

Isaiah says *Oh that thou wouldest rend the heavens, that thou wouldest come down, that the mountains might flow down at thy presence,* **Isaiah 64:1** and in

Isaiah 64:3 he prays *When thou didst awesome things which we looked not for, thou camest down, the mountains flowed down at thy presence.*

Isaiah knew the Lord does come down. This time Isaiah says you come down Lord to make thy name known to thine enemies (verse 2 of chapter 64).

The name of the Lord was seen in what God did – in the awesome things that God does, then and now.

God coming down for man is awesome, it is awesome grace. It is communion with God, above the mercy seat!

All that God does, relates to His name. God's name is a definition of His character.

This Isaiah knew so well. The Lord does not come down in the manner and the way we understand and know of coming down. His presence makes things happen.

God is Omni-present. But He shows Himself in the manner and ways that correspond to our need and His name.

The Bible says of this God, in **Proverbs 30:4** *Who hath ascended up into heaven, or descended? who hath gathered the wind in his fists? who hath bound the waters in a garment? who hath established all the ends*

Psalms 89:34 *My covenant will I not break, nor alter the thing that is gone out of my lips.*

of the earth? what is his name, and what is his son's name, if thou canst tell?

John would, centuries later, state *And no man hath ascended up to heaven, but he that came down from heaven, even the Son of man which is in heaven.* **John 3:13.**

Nahum 1:7 says *The LORD is good, a strong hold in the day of trouble; and he knoweth them that trust in him.* And Solomon would say in **Proverbs 30:** [5] *Every word of God is pure: he is a shield unto them that put their trust in him.*

In God we are fully covered.

In God, we have enough. Enough so that God's character is evident in our lives. Enough for us to glorify the God of all our situations.

The nature and character of the Son of God, whom Solomon refers when he asks *who can tell* – is so humble we cannot know Him if we were to just bump into Him.

Just how good a cover is, is never known until the time and day comes, when the cover is wanted; as soon as possible, at your earliest convenience, until it is wanted as soon as yesterday.

John the Baptist says in **John 1:33,** *"I did not recognize Him, but He who sent me to baptize in water said to me, 'He upon whom you see the Spirit descending and* *remaining upon Him, this is the One who baptizes in the Holy Spirit.'*

This is the nature God seeks from us and expects of us. We cannot walk with shoulders high because God was merciful. We have all sinned and no one is really better than the other, and the Lord will come down for any one, any time, any place, as long as one believes.

It needed God Himself to introduce His Son, Jesus, to John the Baptist. If John could not recognize Him, how then did Jesus walk, how did He interact, how did He speak?

This is Jesus, our cover. He made Himself like one of us so that He could reach all of us.

Jesus was so like us the Jews of His time asked *And they said, is not this Jesus, the son of Joseph, whose father and mother we know? how is it then that he saith, I came down from heaven?* **John 6:42.**

John would say *For the bread of God is he which cometh down from heaven, and giveth life unto the world.* **John 6:33**

When we relate to God and to His Son as the bread of life – we know we need God daily. In the absence of God, we fall and never stand again, we sleep and never wake up, in the absence of this bread, our cognitive

Psalms **89:34** *My covenant will I not break, nor alter the thing that is gone out of my lips.*

ability is lost, and in the absence of this food we are malnourished in every aspect of our lives.

Jesus then confirms the assertions of John in **John 6:38,** Jesus says *For I came down from heaven, not to do mine own will, but the will of him that sent me.*

What Jesus says makes us uncomfortable, because we are not used to Godliness. The Bible says in **John 6:41,** *The Jews then murmured at him, because he said, I am the bread which came down from heaven.*

This is who we are. In plain sight of God we say He is not what He says, yet we see Him live what He says.

When He is down with us, sitting and eating with us, we do not believe. What and how would we have received Him if He had not come down – to our level, so that we could greet Him in the physical, see Him in the physical and touch His garments – in the physical?

The children of Israel who saw Him in the physical still could not believe.

It takes God to introduce His Son to us, just like He did to John the Baptist, if we are to know His Son as He is, our deliverer.

As John would say in **John 6:50,** *This (Jesus) is the bread which cometh down from heaven, that a man may eat thereof, and not die.*

And in **John 6:51** Jesus says *I am the living bread which came down from heaven: if any man eat of this bread, he shall live forever: and the bread that I will give is my flesh, which I will give for the life of the world.*

Strange. How is that possible? Yet it is so true. It is The Truth. It is the gospel. It is "crazy stuff" to those that do not believe.

And in **John 6:58** *This is that bread which came down from heaven: not as your fathers did eat manna, and are dead: he that eateth of this bread shall live forever.*

The challenge with humanity is we want to relate everything to the physical, to the earthly. We want to see and feel the wounds.

This truth about Jesus is not a subject for intellectual debate; it is inconceivable in the realm of the physical. Jesus is the Son of God. He is the way to God. He is the mediator, He stands in the breach, and He is the bridge to heaven.

If we cannot see heaven in the physical, if we cannot see God's throne in the physical, we cannot also see Jesus, the bridge, in the physical. It is spiritual. It is divine. It is eternal, it is infinite. It is understanding Godliness.

John was right and still is right. The bread is different. God called His Son bread, so that we could understand. The language of bread is so central to our lives. The

Psalms 89:34 *My covenant will I not break, nor alter the thing that is gone out of my lips.*

bread that the children of Israel ate, the bread that we eat, almost every day, is sugar full. It has to be eaten in moderation, that is why the Bible says those who ate and who eat the bread we know, will die.

Jesus the bread of life will and should be a part of us, part of our nature, in the physical, the spiritual, the social and the mental. Of life means without Him, there is no life, whichever way you look at it, now and in the future. Without Jesus, there is nothing to look forward to.

When we relate to Jesus the bread of life, the more we relate the better we become, we cannot deteriorate and die; we can only grow and flourish. The more of Jesus we have, the better.

With Jesus, we pray more fervently, we believe more fully. With Jesus, tomorrow is always better than yesterday, regardless of what we meet, regardless of how our circumstances change. For better for worse, Jesus is always better.

This is Jesus, whom Paul alludes to in **Ephesians 4:10** , when Paul says *He that descended is the same also that ascended up far above all heavens, that he might fill all things.*

The thief on the cross failed to see who Jesus was, failed to see what Jesus meant. The thief on the cross says, as reported by Matthew *And saying, Thou that destroyest the temple, and buildest it in three days, save thyself. If thou be the Son of God, come down from the cross.* **Mathew 27:40** .

The thief goes on, *He saved others; himself he cannot save. If he be the King of Israel, let him now come down from the cross, and we will believe him.* **Matthew 27:42**

This is what we say, this is what we do. Our actions tell the same story, our thinking is; Jesus does not matter. We are hanging and the same Jesus also hung. So it does not matter. What is the difference?

We are oblivious, unaware, unconscious, unmindful, ignorant and insensible, to the Godliness of the Son. We have decided if He could come to our level, then He is at our level.

The writers of the gospels all write on this incident. One life was lost, and one life, both hanging on their own crosses, was won over for eternity.

The thief that got lost failed and refused to see, that the cross of Jesus was different. Yes they had been hung "together" with Christ, but the thief failed to reason, to even ask – why are there so many soldiers on this particular cross, why is there such a commotion on and about Jesus? That thinking, that question, would have had a very simple answer – Jesus was different, He was not like them, He was the Son of God.

The questions the thief could have asked were many. All would have had one answer. Even after the sun failed to shine, even after the rocks and the mountains quaked,

Psalms 89:34 *My covenant will I not break, nor alter the thing that is gone out of my lips.*

even after, even after... The Bible does not say that this thief, ever acknowledged Jesus.

The Lord is merciful. He says let us reason together – it may be that we may see who Jesus is. It might be that we may believe, that Jesus is the Son of God. It may be that we may know, Jesus is the only way to the Father, the Creator of the Universe, the Giver of Life.

Jesus could have come down from that cross. Jesus could have answered back, Jesus could have asked the Father for a miracle, but Jesus never did.

His word, His voice, carries more weight than the entire universe put together. The Father and the Son and The Holy Spirit, spoke and all stood fast, they commanded, and everything was established in its place, for all time, until, one day He comes back!

Jesus came and comes down to be our healer. Great multitudes followed Jesus. They were not compelled, they were not forced, and they came because they wanted to relate to this man. Some did not know who He was, some did not understand, but they just wanted to be there, where this man was, this man, called Jesus.

Luke 6:17 says *And he came down with them, and stood in the plain, and the company of his disciples, and a great multitude of people out of all Judaea and Jerusalem, and from the sea coast of Tyre and Sidon, which came to hear him, and to be healed of their diseases;*

Jesus healed all. Many that believed in Him and many that did not. Getting healed was not the big deal. Jesus heals even those that mock him, just so they may know that the leaves they are wearing are temporary raiment, regardless of their nature.

There are as many diseases as there are human beings, at any point in time. We are skin sick and we are bone sick, we are head sick and we are foot sick. Everything about us is sick.

We may all look the same. But those that believe in Jesus, as the way to the Father, and all that do not, are different. Our illness is also never the same, even though it may be called by the same name.

Because every one of us is ill, because every one of us is sick, it simply does not mean we are the same. Every one of us may be coughing, but the cough is just different.

A cough in Jane is never the same as a cough in Mary. Jane and Mary are different, because what drives them, what guides them, what motivates them, what pushes them, what encourages them, is different, they believe differently.

What we believe makes us different. Jesus, makes the difference. The power of the presence of the Lord, makes the difference.

Psalms 89:34 *My covenant will I not break, nor alter the thing that is gone out of my lips.*

Only the presence of Jesus can heal, fully and completely. Sometimes we do not even know the sickness is that great, until Jesus shows us just how sick we are.

The way we speak is sick, the way we walk is sick, the way we do things, everything, is sick. The way we think is worse, God help us.

Thank God, Jesus covers all.

It is foolish, unwise, silly, senseless, and even irrational, to try and heal ourselves. Even though we can see we are so sick, and we do not want to be sick, or at least not that sick. First, because Jesus hung on the cross for us, and second, because we cannot, we have no capacity. The will is not even there as well.

Even if we tried, we cannot lift a finger to heal or cleanse ourselves. The word of God makes us see, the word of God gives us the eyes, so we can see. We are so dirty it stinks, but we cannot do anything on our own. We need the Son of God, and Jesus is His name.

We need His blood. We need the blood of Jesus.

Jesus will come, with His towels, with His wet wipes, all soaked with and in His blood, and wash away everything, every stinking vomit, every rotting and rotten filth. Jesus will wash us squeaky clean. No one else could, no one else would. Jesus does, because He just loves that much.

That is why David would say in **Psalms103** *Bless the LORD, O my soul: and all that is within me, bless his holy name. [2] Bless the LORD, O my soul, and forget not all his benefits: [3] Who forgiveth all thine iniquities; who healeth all thy diseases; [4] Who redeemeth thy life from destruction; who crowneth thee with lovingkindness and tender mercies; [5] Who satisfieth thy mouth with good things; so that thy youth is renewed like the eagle's. [6] The LORD executeth righteousness and judgment for all that are oppressed....[7] He made known his ways unto Moses, his acts unto the children of Israel. [8] The LORD is merciful and gracious, slow to anger, and plenteous in mercy.[9] He will not always chide: neither will he keep his anger forever. [10] He hath not dealt with us after our sins; nor rewarded us according to our iniquities. [11] For as the heaven is high above the earth, so great is his mercy toward them that fear him. [12] As far as the east is from the west, so far hath he removed our transgressions from us. [13] Like as a father pitieth his children, so the LORD pitieth them that fear him. [14] For He knoweth our frame; he remembereth that we are dust.*

The Lord covers all, in time and space. David is recognized as the greatest king of Israel, yet even he could not fathom what this world was about, given just how many diseases he had, not just physical, but spiritual, social and mental.

Psalms 89:34 *My covenant will I not break, nor alter the thing that is gone out of my lips.*

David failed to think right against his general Uriah; David failed to see right against Bathsheba. His mind and his eyes, that time, were spiritually sick.

We are not any better. David says *¹⁷ But the mercy of the LORD is from everlasting to everlasting upon them that fear him, and his righteousness unto children's children; ¹⁸ To such as keep his covenant, and to those that remember his commandments to do them. ¹⁹ The LORD hath prepared his throne in the heavens; and his kingdom ruleth over all.* **Psalms 103.**

Paul would say to king Agrippa, in **Acts 26:9** *I verily thought with myself, that I ought to do many things contrary to the name of Jesus of Nazareth. ¹⁰ Which thing I also did in Jerusalem: and many of the saints did I shut up in prison, having received authority from the chief priests; and when they were put to death, I gave my voice against them. ¹¹ And I punished them oft in every synagogue, and compelled them to blaspheme; and being exceedingly mad against them, I persecuted them even unto strange cities.*

Paul told his story, and David did. Whatever they had done before they met Christ, before they were converted, before they prayed, God forgave, because Jesus covered all.

━━━ *Chapter 7* ━━━

Deliberate Delay

The Psalmist says in **Psalms 113** *Praise ye the LORD. Praise, O ye servants of the LORD, praise the name of the LORD....³ From the rising of the sun unto the going down of the same the LORD's name is to be praised.*

There is no life outside God. There is no existence, there is no substance, there is no being, and there is no time, outside God.

The psalmist, through the experiences of life, knew that very well. He could only say, praise the Lord, praise the Lord. He, like many who have seen, felt and touched the works of the Lord, in their lives, cannot explain.

Psalms 89:34 *My covenant will I not break, nor alter the thing that is gone out of my lips.*

The psalmist suggests we need to praise the Lord at all times and in all places, from the rising of the sun to the setting of the sun.

This is a statement not many can speak, because we believe we are, yet we are not, outside God. That is why the Bible would say, twice, in the psalms, that only fools will say there is no God.

The Bible says in **Psalm 14:1** *The fool hath said in his heart, There is no God. They are corrupt, they have done abominable works, there is none that doeth good.*

And again in **Psalm 53:1**

There is no other god worthy of our praise. Only the Lord God, the Creator of the Universe, the Giver of Life.

When Lazarus, Mary and Martha welcomed Jesus in their home, when they believed what He said, when they followed Him, they never knew one day, a very fine one day, it will be them and Jesus.

The other disciples, the other followers, the others, would just not matter.

Mary and Martha, would, one day, echo what the psalmist said in **Psalms 113:4** *The LORD is high above all nations, and his glory above the heavens. ⁵ Who is like unto the LORD our God, who dwelleth on high, ⁶ Who humbleth himself to behold the things that are in*

heaven, and in the earth! ⁷ He raiseth up the poor out of the dust, and lifteth the needy out of the dunghill; ⁸ That he may set him with princes, even with the princes of his people.

When the Lord sees you, everything changes. The All-seeing God will take time to see you. He knows you, He knows me, by name.

Mary and Martha had been with Jesus, they had eaten from the same plate (Jews do), they had broken bread together. Mary and Martha had heard Jesus pray, they had heard Him teach and preach, but one day, they saw Jesus raise their brother from the dead.

They would see this not as the woman did whose son was raised from the dead, they would see Jesus in their own special way – a dead for four days brother brought to life.

Martha and Mary would know that when the Lord sees your agony, things cannot remain the same. Jesus could have said the word that would have raised Lazarus, like He did in healing the centurion's servant, but Jesus chose to go and call out.

That is why Paul then says to the Thessalonians in **1 Thessalonians 4:16**, *For the Lord himself shall descend from heaven with a shout, with the voice of the archangel, and with the trump of God: and the dead in Christ shall rise first:*

The call is purposeful, it is not random. It is a call to eternity.

Psalms 89:34 *My covenant will I not break, nor alter the thing that is gone out of my lips.*

One sick man reported by John took up a whole chapter. To me, the other sicknesses and diseases reported in the bible did not carry the same weight that the story of Lazarus did. Other illnesses were healed, Lazarus was raised. Lazarus was not raised like the young widow's son, before burial, he was raised after the swell of death, after the stink of death, after the rot of death.

The Bible does not say what illness Lazarus had, it only says, in **John 11,** *Now a certain man was sick, named Lazarus, of Bethany, the town of Mary and her sister Martha.*

Whatever disease Lazarus had, it killed Him, before Jesus came.

A lot of things will die when Jesus is not there. The love, the expectation, the hope, the joy, the peace – everything.

Thank God the sisters to Lazarus had sent word to Jesus. Everything was sick. It does not matter what effort we put, we do not have the power to give life, not to man, not to anything!

Before Jesus comes through, our marriages are dead, our relationships are dead, our children are dead. We only live when Jesus comes our way. It happened to Lazarus.

This Gaither song led by Joy Gardner, sums up a death situation:

A hand of fear gripped the crowd

That day at Jairus' home
When the doctor shook his head
and said she's gone
You could feel that mother's heart break
You could hear them cry and mourn
Their little girl was only twelve years old

Somewhere in the distance
Outlined against the sun
There came a Man on a mission
From the throne
They said "look somebody's coming"
But what they did not know
It was their Promise coming down
that dusty road

There's a Promise coming down that dusty road
From His holy hand healing virtue flows
He's got the keys to what you need
Death and hell He will defeat
There's a Promise coming down that dusty road

The wonder turned to mocking
When Jesus did speak
'Cause He said your daughter's not dead
She's just asleep
Then He turned to the unbelievers
And He told them all "go home"
They heard Him say
"Leave Me and death alone."

Psalms 89:34 *My covenant will I not break, nor alter the thing that is gone out of my lips.*

And then He laid His hand upon the child
And He looked death right in the eye
He said, "All power in Heaven
and earth it belongs to me"
And with a voice that sounds like thunder
He hurled death and hell He will defeat
Oh there's a promise coming down your dusty road

There's a Promise coming down that dusty road
From His holy hand healing virtue flows
He's got the keys to what you need
Death and hell He will defeat
There's a Promise coming down that dusty road

Thank God there was Mary, in verse 2, who knew there was a man named Jesus. The man who can challenge death in all its forms. Mary could have heard about Jairus's daughter, but she probably was not sure – what of Lazarus – dead for four days?

We do not have prior record, where Jesus announced that He loved Lazarus, but my thinking is, Mary knew, Jesus was love, and Jesus could heal her brother.

Mary's experience before the stone throwers was such that she was left with one understanding of Jesus – He cares, and He loves. Mary knew, there was just something about Jesus, which no other man had – Jesus had loving command power.

This love was not conditional; this love was beyond human comprehension. This love was divine.

Of this Mary, the Bible says in **John 8,** *Jesus went unto the mount of Olives. ² And early in the morning he came again into the temple, and all the people came unto him; and he sat down, and taught them. ³ And the scribes and Pharisees brought unto him a woman taken in adultery; and when they had set her in the midst, ⁴ They say unto him, Master, this woman was taken in adultery, in the very act. ⁵ Now Moses in the law commanded us, that such should be stoned: but what sayest thou?*

The world is full of people like the scribes and the Pharisees. The accusers of the brethren.

Mary had been caught – fair and good. Moses truly had said such should be stoned. But where was the man?

The scribes and the Pharisees were right, such had to be stoned, but Moses did not say the woman must be stoned. **Leviticus 20:2** had said both man and woman were to be stoned.

Jesus had to set Mary, the woman, free. The scribes and the Pharisees had set the man free. Mary needed Jesus to free her. She was not just free from being stoned; she had been freed through and through. She had been freed in deed. Mary was new.

Jesus did not ask the scribes and the Pharisees where the man caught in adultery was. Jesus is concerned about

---

Psalms 89:34 *My covenant will I not break, nor alter the thing that is gone out of my lips.*

those that come to him. Screaming or not, that does not matter. What matters is that they came to Jesus. The scribes and the Pharisees were right, only Jesus could judge the matter.

Our God is a fair God. It is His nature, it is His character. The Bible says those that came to Him, He did not reject. He sets free, for free. The past is gone, the future is yours.

And this woman was freed in the temple. Jesus had to write a "new law" on the floors of the temple. Jesus had to write the law of forgiveness, the law of love, regardless.

This is huge; loving regardless, forgiving regardless. Jesus had said, learn of me. That was His law, learn of Him.

If Jesus forgave, the one greater than Solomon, the one greater than the temple, what can man do?

Jesus wrote another law, check first where you are before you say. So true, how is it the fallen are trodden on, when they are supposed to be raised.

This is who we are as people, our thinking is skewed. A fallen brother should never rise again, or so we wish, and to that end we act.

Jesus also wrote – the temple, the house of God, the house of prayer, was for all people. Yes it was right; it was good, it was proper to take Mary to the temple, that is where she really belonged. She had to talk to Jesus.

The scribes and the Pharisees were and are not Jesus. These went to Jesus to accuse Him, but Jesus was waiting for Mary. Jesus is waiting for us all. Jesus is right where we can see Him. He is saying *Come now, let us reason together*.

The Bible says in **John 8:6** *This they said, tempting him, that they might have to accuse him. But Jesus stooped down, and with his finger wrote on the ground, as though he heard them not. So when they continued asking him, he lifted up himself, and said unto them, He that is without sin among you, let him first cast a stone at her.*

Jesus the mediator. He was the judge. The prosecutors were there. A whole lot of them. Jesus did not challenge their doctrine, their code or their creed. Jesus did not challenge their principle. He did not create an intellectual debate. Jesus simply showed them the way.

Jesus did not say Mary was right. Jesus said all have sinned and come short of the glory of God.

John 8:8 says *And again he stooped down, and wrote on the ground. ⁹ And they which heard it, being convicted by their own conscience, went out one by one, beginning at the eldest, even unto the last: and Jesus was left alone, and the woman standing in the midst.*

Psalms 89:34 *My covenant will I not break, nor alter the thing that is gone out of my lips.*

The Bible is plain. Everyone was convicted, by their own conscience. It is a part of us, as people, as Christians. Our conscience speaks, especially as we relate one to another.

John 8:10 goes further *When Jesus had lifted up himself, and saw none but the woman, he said unto her, Woman, where are those thine accusers? hath no man condemned thee? [11] She said, No man, Lord. And Jesus said unto her, Neither do I condemn thee: go, and sin no more.*

David says happy and blessed is the man whose sin is forgiven. And Paul says to the Romans in **Romans 8:1** *There is therefore now no condemnation to them which are in Christ Jesus, who walk not after the flesh but after the spirit.*

Freedom does not come from being with Jesus; it comes from being in Jesus. Jesus is a fountain of living water. Jesus is the light.

Outside Jesus is darkness. Outside Jesus is night, there is gloom. The Bible says in **John 8:12** *Then spake Jesus again unto them, saying, I am the light of the world: he that followeth me shall not walk in darkness, but shall have the light of life. [13] The Pharisees therefore said unto him, Thou bearest record of thyself; thy record is not true. [14] Jesus answered and said unto them, Though I bear record of myself, yet my record is true: for I know whence I came, and whither I go; but ye cannot tell whence I come, and whither I go.*

Wow, what conversation! The scribes and the Pharisees were just living up to expectation. They did not know Jesus. Isaiah was right in **Isaiah 53**, they esteemed Him not, because they just did not know who this man was.

The scribes and the Pharisees saw, they heard, but they still would not believe. And John says in 1 John 1:1 *That which we have seen and heard declare we unto you, that ye also may have fellowship with us: and truly our fellowship is with the Father, and with his Son Jesus Christ.*

John acknowledges that what he saw and heard was of the Father. John, the scribes and the Pharisees all heard the same things, the same that they saw, the same Jesus they touched, but Jesus was their difference.

Jesus was the son of God. John goes further to say in **1 John 3:1** *Behold, what manner of love the Father hath bestowed upon us, that we should be called the sons of God: therefore the world knoweth us not, because it knew him not.*

Thank God the scribes and the Pharisees took Mary to the temple. Jesus would still judge Mary, but not after the flesh, Jesus would judge after the Spirit. Where Jesus judged, the judgement is fair.

In **John 8:15** Jesus says *Ye judge after the flesh; I judge no man.* [16] *And yet if I judge, my judgment is true: for I am not alone, but I and the Father that sent me.* [17] *It is*

Psalms 89:34 *My covenant will I not break, nor alter the thing that is gone out of my lips.*

also written in your law, that the testimony of two men is true. [18] I am one that bear witness of myself, and the Father that sent me beareth witness of me.

This is huge conversation. The scribes and the Pharisees deemed themselves the defenders of God and Godliness.

God does not need us, we need God. They professed to follow the law but never knew who gave that law. Moses would have told them – this is the Creator of the Universe, the Giver of Life. The Son and the Father are one.

All creatures, great and small, are in the palms of His hands. Jesus is the heir apparent!

John 8:19 says *Then said they unto him, Where is thy Father? Jesus answered; Ye neither know me, nor my Father: if ye had known me, ye should have known my Father also. [20] These words spake Jesus in the treasury, as he taught in the temple: and no man laid hands on him; for his hour was not yet come.*

Jesus made conversation in the temple. The place, the building, the scribes and the Pharisees considered their territory, their seat, but it was the place Jesus could fill up, only this time, Jesus was not for show. The scribes and the Pharisees did not and could not, feel the power of the presence of the Lord.

The two men that walked with Jesus after the resurrection, on their way to Emmaus, would also ask one to another, *Did not our heart burn within us, while he talked with us by the way, and while he opened to us the scriptures?* **Luke 24:32**

The power of the presence of the Lord should burn our very being, should make us aware of Godliness. Nothing can remain the same.

John 8:21 says *Then said Jesus again unto them, I go my way, and ye shall seek me, and shall die in your sins: whither I go, ye cannot come.*

Jesus was so sure, if you do not know Him and His Father, then heaven was not for you; if you die in your sins, then heaven is not for you.

Jesus was sure, these guys needed to look for Him and find Him. Outside that they could not go where He would go, where He would be.

Jesus was sure, their ways and His ways went different directions. Jesus gave them the liberty – go your way and I go mine.

But in your state, don't come where I go, you simply do not belong, and you cannot just come.

To go where Jesus goes, there are conditions. Walking with Jesus is a huge thing. Walking with Jesus is Godliness.

Then the Jews would ask *Will he kill himself? Because he saith, whither I go, ye cannot come.* **John 8:22.**

Psalms **89:34** *My covenant will I not break, nor alter the thing that is gone out of my lips.*

Yes. These were the scribes and the Pharisees, that is just the way they think. The gap between the carnal and the heavenly is that big.

Heavenly and Godly things, are only spiritually discerned. Heaven and earth are mutually exclusive, unless we see better, we hear better, we live better, in Jesus, the Son of God, heaven we will not see.

John 8:23 says *And he said unto them, Ye are from beneath; I am from above: ye are of this world; I am not of this world. ²⁴ I said therefore unto you, that ye shall die in your sins: for if ye believe not that I am he, ye shall die in your sins.*

The scribes and the Pharisees should have held back. No more talking. But they would not stop.

Instead, **John 8:25** says *Then said they unto him, Who art thou? And Jesus saith unto them, Even the same that I said unto you from the beginning. ²⁶ I have many things to say and to judge of you: but he that sent me is true; and I speak to the world those things which I have heard of him. ²⁷ They understood not that he spake to them of the Father.*

They did not and they would not, understand. How could they. The scribes and the Pharisees would not, because they are just like us.

In an article, The **Woes of the Pharisees,** quoted as is below, is a list of criticisms by Jesus, against scribes and Pharisees. Scripture referenced is Luke 11:37–

54 and Matthew 23:1–39. Mark   12:35–40 and Luke
20:45–47 also include warnings about scribes.

The woes are mentioned twice in the narratives in the
Gospels of Matthew and Luke.....The woes are all woes
of hypocrisy and illustrate the differences between inner
and outer moral states. Jesus portrays the Pharisees as
impatient with outward, ritual observance of minutiae
which made them look acceptable and virtuous
outwardly but left the inner person unreformed.

The list is generally and arguably listed as follows:

1. They taught about God but did not love God,
2. They preached God but converted people to
    dead religion, thus making those converts twice
    as much sons of hell as they themselves were.
3. They taught swearing by the ornaments of the
    temple.
4. They taught the law but did not practice some
    of the most important parts of the law – justice,
    mercy, faithfulness to God.
5. They presented an appearance of being 'clean'
    (self-restrained, not involved in carnal matters),
    yet they were dirty inside: they seethed with
    hidden worldly desires, carnality. They were
    full of *greed and self-indulgence*.
6. They exhibited themselves as righteous on
    account of being scrupulous keepers of the law,
    but were in fact not righteous: their mask

Psalms 89:34 *My covenant will I not break, nor alter the thing that
is gone out of my lips.*

of righteousness hid a secret inner world of ungodly thoughts and feelings. They were full of wickedness. They were *like whitewashed tombs, beautiful on the outside, but full of dead men's bones.*

7. They professed a high regard for the dead prophets of old, and claimed that they would never have persecuted and murdered prophets, when in fact they were cut from the same cloth as the persecutors and murderers: they too had murderous blood in their veins.

Wikipedia.org. (July, 2018). *Woes of the Pharisees.* [online]. Available at https://en.m.wikipedia.org/wiki/Woes_of_the_Pharisees [Accessed February 23, 2019]

This is an interesting summary of what the Pharisees presumably were. The same as these, would not be quiet when Jesus speaks. The gap between the righteous Jesus and the Pharisees was just too big. Yet Jesus readily makes reference to same.

Jesus says if you want to see God, you need to be better than the Pharisees! How so?

Arguably, Jesus did not mean be more hypocritical than the Pharisees. Jesus meant the Pharisees believe; and we ought to believe more, the Pharisees pray, we ought to pray more. Belief and prayer are "zero-sum games". Either you pray, or you don't, and either you believe, or you don't. Your works will tell.

Jesus was saying, the fervent prayer of a righteous man availed much. The Holy Spirit of the Lord will tell you what to do.

Another article titled **Who were the scribes that often argued with Jesus?** makes interesting reading. To the question, the answer is given:

Scribes in ancient Israel were learned men whose business was to study the Law, transcribe it, and write commentaries on it. They were also hired on occasions when the need for a written document arose or when an interpretation of a legal point was needed. Ezra, "a teacher well versed in the Law of Moses," was a scribe (**Ezra7:6**).

The scribes took their job of preserving Scripture very seriously; they would copy and recopy the Bible meticulously, even counting letters and spaces to ensure each copy was correct. We can thank the Jewish scribes for preserving the Old Testament portion of our Bibles.

Jews became increasingly known as "the people of the Book" because of their faithful study of Scripture, particularly the Law and how it should be followed. In the New Testament era, scribes were often associated with the sect of the Pharisees, although not all Pharisees were scribes (see **Matthew 5:20; 12:38**).

Psalms 89:34 *My covenant will I not break, nor alter the thing that is gone out of my lips.*

They were teachers of the people (**Mark 1:22**) and interpreters of the Law. They were widely respected by the community because of their knowledge, dedication, and outward appearance of Law-keeping.

The scribes went beyond interpretation of Scripture, however, and added many man-made traditions to what God had said. They became professionals at spelling out the letter of the Law while ignoring the spirit behind it. Things became so bad that the regulations and traditions the scribes added to the Law were considered more important than the Law itself. This led to many confrontations between Jesus and the Pharisees and scribes. At the beginning of the Sermon on the Mount, Jesus shocked His audience by declaring that the righteousness of the scribes was not enough to get anyone to heaven (**Matthew 5:20**). A large portion of Jesus' sermon then dealt with what the people had been taught (by the scribes) and what God actually wanted (**Matthew 5:21–48**). Toward the end of Jesus' ministry, He thoroughly condemned the scribes for their hypocrisy (**Matthew 23**). They knew the Law, and they taught it to others, but they did not obey it.

The scribes' original aim was in earnest—to know and preserve the Law and encourage others to keep it. But things turned horribly wrong when man-made traditions overshadowed God's Word and a pretense of holiness replaced a life of true Godliness. The scribes, whose stated goal was to preserve the Word, actually *nullified* it by the traditions they handed down (**Mark7:13**).

How did things get so far off course? Probably because the Jews, after surviving centuries of persecution and enslavement, clung in pride to the keeping of the Law and how it marked them as God's chosen people. The Jews of Jesus' day certainly had an attitude of superiority (**John 7:49**), which Jesus opposed (**Matthew 9:12**). The bigger problem was that the scribes were hypocrites at heart. They were more interested in appearing good to men than they were in pleasing God. Eventually, it was these same scribes who played a part in having Jesus arrested and crucified (**Matthew 26:57; Mark 15:1; Luke 22:1–2**).

The lesson every Christian can learn from the hypocrisy of the scribes is that God wants more than outward acts of righteousness. He wants an inward change of heart that is constantly yielding in love and obedience to Christ.

https://www.gotquestions.org/scribes-Jesus.html

Jesus dealt with the scribes and He dealt with the Pharisees, the whole 42 months of His ministry, challenging their way of doing things, their beliefs, and their doctrine. Jesus challenged their life and how they lived.

Jesus challenged their sight and their hearing. Jesus shook their foundations. Jesus says in **John 8:28.........** *When ye have lifted up the Son of man, then shall ye*

Psalms 89:34 *My covenant will I not break, nor alter the thing that is gone out of my lips.*

know that I am he, and that I do nothing of myself; but as my Father hath taught me, I speak these things. [29] And he that sent me is with me: the Father hath not left me alone; for I do always those things that please him. [30] As he spake these words, many believed on him.

Jesus knew these guys were going to crucify Him. They were going to lift Him up on Calvary's mountain, on the cross. It would be then, that these guys would know – it was Him!

The Bible says many believed Jesus when Jesus spoke. But those that sought to challenge His authority never did.

Was it good for you and me? Yes it was. Jesus had to be raised on Mount Calvary; He had to be raised on the good old rugged cross, so that you, and I, could also know, that it was He.

No one is left out, and no one was left out. Even those that crucified Jesus had a chance; they had opportunity to believe, because the Father came down for His Son. The centurion told the story, Pilate the governor did, and the soldiers who guarded the tomb did, perhaps not publicly, but privately.

Jesus says to the scribes and the Pharisees, when YOU have lifted me up, then YOU will know that all I said is true, everything that I said, from the beginning.

They sure did plan to lift Him up. They needed a cause, they needed a reason, and they found it after Lazarus was raised from the dead!

John 8:31 says *Then said Jesus to those Jews which believed on him, If ye continue in my word, then are ye my disciples indeed; ³² And ye shall know the truth, and the truth shall make you free. ³³ They answered him, We be Abraham's seed, and were never in bondage to any man: how sayest thou, Ye shall be made free?*

Even those that had believed Him still had questions. Now it was not about Moses, it was about Abraham.

This was Jesus, before Abraham was, He was. When faith and belief was imputed in Abraham as righteousness, it was the Trinity – God the Father, God the Holy Spirit and Jesus the Christ, the Son of God, who gave to Abraham the title – father of many nations. It was they who gave Isaac to Abraham.

Abraham just believed. These sons of Abraham could not and did not. Jesus was not going to force them to believe. He could have done something, anything, to make them see, to make them believe, but He did not. It is His nature, He does not force, but He just loves – beyond measure.

John 8:34 says *Jesus answered them, Verily, verily, I say unto you, Whosoever committeth sin is the servant of sin. ³⁵ And the servant abideth not in the house for* *ever: but the Son abideth ever. ³⁶ If the Son therefore shall make you free, ye shall be free indeed.*

Jesus is saying, sin takes away your honour. Sin makes you work. To achieve and to be recognized, yet not recognized nor achieving. What a servant thinks he has attained, realized, accomplished, completed, or just done well, it is for the glory of another.

Servants are not at equal with their employers. That, the children of Israel, the earlier generation of these scribes and Pharisees, knew very well.

They had been servants in Egypt, even though they still lived in the land of Goshen. They should have known better, what freedom meant.

Goshen was good, when Joseph was alive and in charge. When Joseph died, Goshen was still there, it was still good, but the children of Israel had changed status. The privilege had gone, the recognition was gone, and they were now slaves.

It does not matter where you stay, Goshen or other; sin can make you its slave, there.

The Lord had said to Isaiah; let them know I plucked them out of Egypt on eagle's wings (Exodus 19:4). Getting freedom comes with serious sacrifice. Someone pays, but these Jews had forgotten, or did their parents not teach them?

The memorials of stone that their parents heaped on crossing the Jordan they would not remember. God had said, the memorials were for all generations. God knew they would forget.

But this generation had forgotten. Loss of memory is never a good thing. Jesus replies in

John 8:37 *I know that ye are Abraham's seed; but ye seek to kill me, because my word hath no place in you. [38] I speak that which I have seen with my Father: and ye do that which ye have seen with your father. [39] They answered and said unto him, Abraham is our father. Jesus saith unto them, If ye were Abraham's children, ye would do the works of Abraham.*

What we do as people, is just a reflection of where we come from. Unless the Lord intervenes, truly nothing good will come out of Nazareth.

When the Lord is in us and in it, whatever it is, even forgotten towns and cities like Bethlehem of Judea, small and insignificant, we become the source of victory, freedom, sanity and everything divine.

Micah says in **5:2** God's origins are of old. Jesus is the Son of God. The Bible says *[2] But thou, Bethlehem Ephratah, though thou be little among the thousands of Judah, yet out of thee shall he come forth unto me that is to be ruler in Israel; whose goings forth have been from of old, from everlasting.*

These scribes and Pharisees, never knew, the origins of Jesus. Jesus was older than His age!

Psalms 89:34 *My covenant will I not break, nor alter the thing that is gone out of my lips.*

Jesus implores in **John 8:40** *But now ye seek to kill me, a man that hath told you the truth, which I have heard of God: this did not Abraham. ⁴¹ Ye do the deeds of your father. Then said they to him, We be not born of fornication; we have one Father, even God. ⁴² Jesus said unto them, If God were your Father, ye would love me: for I proceeded forth and came from God; neither came I of myself, but he sent me. ⁴³ Why do ye not understand my speech? even because ye cannot hear my word.*

I read verse 43 and thought – this is not good.

Jesus had to explain. They could not understand what Jesus was saying, because their father would not have understood. He was cast down from heaven, because he could not understand the principles of God. Their father could not understand the power, the love and the majesty of the Father, the Creator of the Universe, and The Giver of Life.

These children needed to be born again – of a different Father. The person you call father is very important. The blood in your veins has a lot of bearing on the outcomes of and in your life. The blood in your veins says who you are. The blood in your veins gives you an identity.

To change parentage – one just needs to be born again!

Jesus says in **John 8:44** *Ye are of your father the devil, and the lusts of your father ye will do. He was a murderer from the beginning, and abode not in the truth, because there is no truth in him. When he speaketh a lie,* *he speaketh of his own: for he is a liar, and the father of it.*

Jesus was there. He was there then, and He is here still. Jesus is eternal. Jesus knew the scribes, He knew the Pharisees, and Jesus knew their father.

Jesus goes on *And because I tell you the truth, ye believe me not. [46] Which of you convinceth me of sin? And if I say the truth, why do ye not believe me? [47] He that is of God heareth God's words: ye therefore hear them not, because ye are not of God.* **John 8:45**

Jesus was preaching. Jesus was calling a spade a spade. Jesus was firm, Jesus was eloquent, Jesus was logical.

Jesus was saying you cannot attribute any sin to me, yet when I speak, you cannot believe me. Jesus gives them a chance for them to feel good about themselves. Jesus says, it is really not your fault; you are just children of a bad father.

Why, because your project, your works, are for the enemy. You cannot distinguish right from wrong. The scribes and the Pharisees had a project. It was called "accuse".

Jesus was saying the scribes and the Pharisees believed themselves right and all others wrong. This was Jesus speaking, because your father is the devil and lying is his nature. He can never speak truth; he can never see truth, because there is no truth in him.

Psalms 89:34 *My covenant will I not break, nor alter the thing that is gone out of my lips.*

Were the scribes and the Pharisees on some kind of show? Possibly. But no, they had a mission; they had to lift up Christ!

John 8:48 says *Then answered the Jews, and said unto him, Say we not well that thou art a Samaritan, and hast a devil? ⁴⁹ Jesus answered, I have not a devil; but I honour my Father, and ye do dishonour me. ⁵⁰ And I seek not mine own glory: there is one that seeketh and judgeth. ⁵¹ Verily, verily, I say unto you, If a man keep my saying, he shall never see death.*

Jesus preached on. The Jews would not understand. First it was about Moses, and then it was about Abraham, now it was about the Samaritans.

That was and still is the way sinful man think. It is all much skewed thinking. It is tilted, it is slanted, it is twisted, it is crooked thinking.

It did not matter how Jesus would preach, the scribes were scribes and the Pharisees were Pharisees.

They would not change unless the blood changed. They needed the blood that spoke better things than that of Abel, according to the book of Hebrews. They needed this very same Jesus, what irony!

The Bible says in **John 8:52** *Then said the Jews unto him, Now we know that thou hast a devil. Abraham is dead, and the prophets; and thou sayest, If a man keep my saying, he shall never taste of death. ⁵³ Art thou*

greater than our father Abraham, which is dead? and
the prophets are dead: whom makest thou thyself?*

The questions the Jews asked were all consistent with
their knowledge.

These were the type of people that believed after the
event, people who would close the stable door after the
horse has bolted. And Jesus was right, when they had
lifted up Jesus, they would know – it was He.

This is the fall out that we have with God, with His Son
and His Holy Spirit. When the word of God speaks, we
have closed our ears. We have given ourselves over to
unbelief.

John 8:54 says *Jesus answered, If I honour myself, my
honour is nothing: it is my Father that honoureth me; of
whom ye say, that he is your God: ⁵⁵ Yet ye have not
known him; but I know him: and if I should say, I know
him not, I shall be a liar like unto you: but I know him,
and keep his saying. ⁵⁶ Your father Abraham rejoiced to
see my day: and he saw it, and was glad.*

Yes, the father honoured our Saviour. Jesus was given
all power, in heaven and on earth; Jesus was given a
name, which is above every other name.

Jesus sits at the right hand of the Father.

The Bible says *Then said the Jews unto him, Thou art
not yet fifty years old, and hast thou seen Abraham?*

Psalms **89:34** *My covenant will I not break, nor alter the thing that
is gone out of my lips.*

[58] Jesus said unto them, Verily, verily, I say unto you, Before Abraham was, I am. **John 8:57**

They saw Jesus; they recognized the son of Joseph and Mary. They could identify the brother of James, but they did not know my Jesus. They could not discern my deliverer, my healer, my Lord Protector.

Yes, they asked the questions, and Jesus answered, just as He would, to you and to me. But Jesus was never their equal. Jesus was the Son of God. Jesus had and has everlastingness in His blood.

Yes, before Abraham was, Jesus was. This is the confidence that we have, that with Jesus, we can weather any storm, we can ride any tide. Because Jesus is the former of all things.

With Jesus, we are not mere mortals; we are adopted, and belong to the infinite of Godliness. We are also sons of God.

Jesus is our brother, only He sticks closer than a brother. It does not matter how tall or how fat the challenge, Jesus walks us through.

John 8:59 says *Then took they up stones to cast at him: but Jesus hid himself, and went out of the temple, going through the midst of them, and so passed by.*

This is Jesus, either we believe Him or reject Him. Whatever we do, will have consequences!

In this chapter of John, God had created an opportunity for His Son – to speak, to preach, to challenge.

Even in our lives, there are times we have had to hide. The stones are many and everywhere.

Thank God, for in Jesus we can also hide. In Jesus we are delivered, in Jesus we are covered. We only need to let Jesus know, where we stand – for Him or against Him.

At times, we also carry stones. As soon as we depart and or go far away from God, carrying stones becomes part of who we are.

We need to take time, take time off, to know, to understand, what Jesus means to you, to me, to life, present and eternal.

It does not matter the size of the stone, big or small, a stone is a stone, it hurts.

The scribes and the Pharisees wanted to stone Mary, and Mary found refuge in Jesus, then the scribes and the Pharisees, together with the rest of the Jews in the temple, turned their fury, to Jesus.

Jesus is our hiding place; He is our City of refuge, our strong tower. Running to Jesus, we are safe. If Jesus hid from the stones of the scribes and the Pharisees, if Jesus

Psalms 89:34 *My covenant will I not break, nor alter the thing that is gone out of my lips.*

rescued Mary from the stones, He can and He will, hide YOU and He can hide ME too.

This Jesus, will fill up any temple, He will write His law, in your heart and in my heart, ever stronger every day. Those that see, will never know what Jesus wrote, but they will know, Jesus wrote, on your heart and mine too, on our minds, and on our lives, on our situations, on our circumstances. Because Jesus writes, what we can read, and what others can see.

Mary would not have probably run to Jesus on her own, believing herself very sinful. Those that introduced Mary to Jesus were not even believers.

They went to Jesus because they wanted Jesus not only to condemn Mary, but also to tempt Jesus.

But Jesus was up and above. He was connected with heaven. Jesus did not shout at the scribes and the Pharisees, Jesus simply wrote – on the floor of the temple.

Back to Lazarus: Human beings love what will benefit them, human beings love for profit, but Jesus just loves, His very being is love.

That realization sent the sisters Mary and Martha running to Jesus. They chose to pursue Jesus and all He stood for. Martha and Mary fully believed, that Jesus could and Jesus would, if only He was on time!

It is interesting that God preferred to use Mary to illustrate that Jesus had power over death.

The Bible says in **John 11: 4** *When Jesus heard that, he said, This sickness is not unto death, but for the glory of God, that the Son of God might be glorified thereby.*

The scripture gives an impression Jesus was saying Lazarus was not going to die. But no, Lazarus actually died, and was buried.

My thinking is, when Jesus said this *sickness is not unto death*, Jesus was preaching to the disciples and to us. There are things that will happen in our lives, which may appear to have killed us, but are all grace coated.

The way we feel says we are dead, others who see us can say we are dead, but Jesus says, no, not so fast, it is not always the way it looks.

How those situations end up will then depend on who is called to attend to our seemingly dead situations. I would call Jesus, like Mary did.

This is the same Jesus who said to the disciples of John; go tell John the Baptist, what you saw. The Bible records *Then Jesus answering said unto them, Go your way, and tell John what things ye have seen and heard; how that the blind see, the lame walk, the lepers are cleansed, the deaf hear, the dead are raised, to the poor the gospel is preached.* **Luke 6:22**

Psalms 89:34 *My covenant will I not break, nor alter the thing that is gone out of my lips.*

Mary and Martha went to Jesus. Jesus had formed a bond with the three siblings, and the Bible acknowledges in verse 5. It is recorded that [5] *Now Jesus loved Martha, and her sister, and Lazarus.*

When Jesus seemingly delays, it does not mean He cares less. His actions are quite deliberate.

The Bible says in verse 6, *When he had heard therefore that he was sick, he abode two days still in the same place where he was.*

This means it took two days to get to Lazarus. When Jesus got to Bethany, Martha said Lazarus had been dead for four days. Jesus started moving after day two.

Is it then possible that Mary and Martha also delayed in telling Jesus? From the reading, and arguably, Lazarus died the day Jesus was told. Or is it that Mary and Martha believed Jesus could just say a word, wherever He was, and Lazarus would live.

Whatever they thought, it was expedient that they told Jesus. Telling Jesus was the most practical thing to do, it was convenient too, it was useful, advantageous, and it was beneficial. It was even politically correct. Telling Jesus was the thing to do – whether or not Lazarus was gasping his last breaths. That did not matter, as long as Jesus knew. Jesus would know what to do.

My thinking is, if Jesus had gone the first time He heard Lazarus was ill, Jesus would have healed Lazarus, He would not have raised Lazarus.

Being healed and being raised are miles apart. It is better to let Jesus raise you than to heal you. Healing is making good, and raising is increasing and promoting. Raising is changing another's position; it is movement, from one level to another.

Raising is lifting. We all want healing, but we all need lifting. The two are not the same. Healing can take me back to the position that I was before, but raising makes everything better, better than before. Raising defies gravity, raising defies the pull of nature.

When Jesus raises, everything is new.

A four day dead body would need new flesh, new skin, and new limbs. A four day old dead body stinks. Only the new can take the stink away.

The world is not concerned when Christians do what the world can do. The world can also heal, but the world cannot raise. Only God does. Even time can heal, time can make us forget, but only God can make new.

Rising is extraordinary. Healing has no consequences, but rising has.

Jesus WILL raise those He loves. This means you, this means I, but there are conditions.

Psalms 89:34 *My covenant will I not break, nor alter the thing that is gone out of my lips.*

The Bible says whosoever calls upon the name of the Lord shall be saved. I want to believe, this also means, whoever calls upon the name of the Lord, shall be raised.

Our God is an equal opportunity God, it does not matter where you come from, or what tag society has given you, if you call on the name of the Lord, you WILL be raised, and you WILL be saved.

Paul says in **Acts 2:21** *And it shall come to pass, that whosoever shall call on the name of the Lord shall be saved.*

Also to the **Romans** in **10:13** *For whosoever shall call upon the name of the Lord shall be saved.*

We just need to be justified, called to be saints, and sanctified, living like saints. The Lord enables, for we have neither the will nor the dignity, the self-respect, of being saintly.

Paul would say in **1 Corinthians 1:2-5** *Unto the church of God which is at Corinth, to them that are sanctified in Christ Jesus, called to be saints, with all that in every place call upon the name of Jesus Christ our Lord,*

The church of God has been called to be saints. Everyone who has an ear has been called. Some just do not care who calls. When you know who is calling you, you know exactly how to respond, to run or to walk, or even to ignore, like you never heard. We all hear, but how we respond is our choice.

Jesus has a bigger program than our daily needs. He cares for the little details of our lives, as much as He cares for the greater good.

What we need is to just trust Him. Jesus is the Son of God. The Bible says in the following verses:

John 11:7 *Then after that saith he to his disciples, Let us go into Judaea again. [8] His disciples say unto him, Master, the Jews of late sought to stone thee; and goest thou thither again? [9] Jesus answered, Are there not twelve hours in the day? If any man walk in the day, he stumbleth not, because he seeth the light of this world. [10] But if a man walk in the night, he stumbleth, because there is no light in him.*

Something had happened in Judea, the Jews had wanted to stone Jesus. The disciples knew Judea was not a good to go area, but Jesus had a friend there, and that friend had a name, Lazarus.

The Bible says in **John 11:11** *These things said he: and after that he saith unto them, Our friend Lazarus sleepeth; but I go, that I may awake him out of sleep. [12] Then said his disciples, Lord, if he sleep, he shall do well. [13] Howbeit Jesus spake of his death: but they thought that he had spoken of taking of rest in sleep. [14] Then said Jesus unto them plainly, Lazarus is dead.*

Psalms 89:34 *My covenant will I not break, nor alter the thing that is gone out of my lips.*

The way Jesus sees issues and things is very different from how man sees.

The disciples had been with Jesus for a while, but even the way Jesus spoke on any one day, they would not understand. Until Jesus makes it plain to us, we are confused and simply cannot see. The fact is, we need Jesus through and through.

Jesus goes on to say *And I am glad for your sakes that I was not there, to the intent ye may believe; nevertheless let us go unto him.* **John 11:15**

Jesus says He was glad He had not been there when Lazarus was sick. Did Jesus know Lazarus was now dead? My thinking is He did, because He already knew the mission – so that we could fully believe. Yes, Jesus was going to Judea for us, so that we could believe in Him a little more.

Our intellect can be an obstruction to the things of God. It is easier for a man who does not have much to believe in God. The not so rich guy will say, hey, I need this Jesus for my next meal, for cover, for everything. The not so poor guy will say, am good to go, I will call Jesus when my plane is taking off and when I am lending.

The truth is Jesus is our everything, with or without private jets, with or without a plate of food on the table.

John 11:16 says *Then said Thomas, which is called Didymus, unto his fellow disciples, Let us also go, that we may die with him.* *[17] Then when Jesus came, he found* *that he had lain in the grave four days already.* ¹⁸ *Now Bethany was nigh unto Jerusalem, about fifteen furlongs off:* ¹⁹ *And many of the Jews came to Martha and Mary, to comfort them concerning their brother.* ²⁰ *Then Martha, as soon as she heard that Jesus was coming, went and met him: but Mary sat still in the house.* ²¹ *Then said Martha unto Jesus, Lord, if thou hadst been here, my brother had not died.* ²² *But I know, that even now, whatsoever thou wilt ask of God, God will give it thee.* ²³ *Jesus saith unto her, Thy brother shall rise again.*²⁴ *Martha saith unto him, I know that he shall rise again in the resurrection at the last day.* ²⁵ *Jesus said unto her, I am the resurrection, and the life: he that believeth in me, though he were dead, yet shall he live:* ²⁶ *And whosoever liveth and believeth in me shall never die. Believest thou this?*

This is where we are. Jesus is the resurrection and the life. It is a true saying. He said it; He is the Son of God.

Martha says in verse 27, *Yea, Lord: I believe that thou art the Christ, the Son of God, which should come into the world,* and

John 11:28 says *And when she had so said, she went her way, and called Mary her sister secretly, saying, The Master is come, and calleth for thee.* ²⁹ *As soon as she heard that, she arose quickly, and came unto him.* ³⁰ *Now Jesus was not yet come into the town, but was in that place where Martha met him.* ³¹ *The Jews then which were with her in the house, and comforted her,*

Psalms 89:34 *My covenant will I not break, nor alter the thing that is gone out of my lips.*

when they saw Mary, that she rose up hastily and went out, followed her, saying, She goeth unto the grave to weep there. ³² *Then when Mary was come where Jesus was, and saw him, she fell down at his feet, saying unto him, Lord, if thou hadst been here, my brother had not died.* ³³ *When Jesus therefore saw her weeping, and the Jews also weeping which came with her, he groaned in the spirit, and was troubled.*

This is our God; He knows the feeling of our infirmities. Mary did not know, that Jesus wipes away all the tears. Jesus says, weep no more, fear no more – I am here, I am He.

In **John 11:34** the Bible says Jesus asks *Where have ye laid him? They said unto him, Lord, come and see.* ³⁵ *Jesus wept.* ³⁶ *Then said the Jews, Behold how he loved him!* ³⁷ ***And some of them said, Could not this man, which opened the eyes of the blind, have caused that even this man should not have died?*** ³⁸ *Jesus therefore again groaning in himself cometh to the grave. It was a cave, and a stone lay upon it.* ³⁹ *Jesus said, Take ye away the stone. Martha, the sister of him that was dead, saith unto him, Lord, by this time he stinketh: for he hath been dead four days.* ⁴⁰ *Jesus saith unto her, Said I not unto thee, that,* ***if thou wouldest believe, thou shouldest see the glory of God?*** ⁴¹ *Then they took away the stone from the place where the dead was laid. And Jesus lifted up his eyes, and said, Father,* ***I thank thee that thou hast heard me.*** ⁴² *And I knew that thou hearest me always: but because of the people which stand by I* *said it, that they may believe that thou hast sent me.* *43 And when he thus had spoken, he cried with a loud voice, Lazarus, come forth. 44 And he that was dead came forth, bound hand and foot with grave clothes: and his face was bound about with a napkin. Jesus saith unto them, Loose him, and let him go.*

It was not about Lazarus, it was about you, it was about me. That we could believe, that Jesus was He, the Son of God.

Many things will have to die before we see God. Some of the things we hold on to are just grave clothes. We are as dead as Lazarus before Jesus came.

Mary, Martha, the Jews, the disciples, must have shouted, must have sung – this is our God, we have waited for Him.

The Bible says, when this Jesus, comes to take His, home, when He comes to take us home, we will shout – this is our God, we have waited for Him.

Isaiah says in **25:9** *And it shall be said in that day, Lo, this is our God; we have waited for him, and he will save us: this is the LORD; we have waited for him, we will be glad and rejoice in his salvation.*

Jesus takes away the grave clothes from our lives. He takes away the hurt and the hate, the bitterness, the unforgiving spirit, the pride, the arrogance, everything.

Psalms 89:34 *My covenant will I not break, nor alter the thing that is gone out of my lips.*

His word is and remains the same – I am the resurrection and the life. This is what John records in **John 11:25** *Jesus said unto her, I am the resurrection, and the life: he that believeth in me, though he were dead, yet shall he live:*

Jesus had to go back to Judea, so that we could understand and believe more, that Jesus indeed was the power behind life. That is why John says without Him was not anything made which was made. **John 1:3**

Jesus went back to Judea for one man, Lazarus.

Jesus went back to Judea for Martha and for Mary.

Jesus went back to Judea for His disciples.

Jesus went back to Judea for John the Baptist, for Thomas.

Jesus went back to Judea for the Jews and the Gentiles.

Jesus went back to Judea for the scribes and the Pharisees.

He went back to Judea for you and for me.

Jesus went back to Judea for people – every nation, kindred, tongue and people.

The Bible says in **John 11:45** *Then many of the Jews which came to Mary, and **had seen the things which Jesus did, believed on him.** [46] But some of them went* *their ways to the Pharisees, and told them what things Jesus had done. [47] Then gathered the chief priests and the Pharisees a council, and said, What do we? for this man doeth many miracles. [48] If we let him thus alone, all men will believe on him: and the Romans shall come and take away both our place and nation. [49] **And one of them, named Caiaphas, being the high priest that same year, said unto them, Ye know nothing at all, [50] Nor consider that it is expedient for us, that one man should die for the people, and that the whole nation perish not.** [51] And this spake he not of himself: but being high priest that year, he prophesied that Jesus should die for that nation; [52] And not for that nation only, but that also he should gather together in one the children of God that were scattered abroad.*

This is the plan of salvation summarized by the high priest, in advertently. Caiaphas was telling the good news, that Christ would die for all, to gather them together for the kingdom of God.

It was a true saying that Jesus had said, the death of Lazarus was a means to an end.

It was expedient that Jesus would die for us. Caiaphas was saying, it was convenient, it was practical, and it was useful, beneficial, advantageous, self-serving, it was politically correct and pragmatic that Jesus (one man) would die for the benefit of many.

Psalms 89:34 *My covenant will I not break, nor alter the thing that is gone out of my lips.*

No other man could have done that. Only Jesus could have died for all. His blood would be an incessant river of love, of power, of strength and courage, of hope and dignity, for all time and for all people.

This was God's plan on track.

John 11:53 says *Then **from that day forth they took counsel together for to put him to death.** [54] Jesus therefore walked no more openly among the Jews; but went thence unto a country near to the wilderness, into a city called Ephraim, and there continued with his disciples. [55] And the Jews' Passover was nigh at hand: and many went out of the country up to Jerusalem before the Passover, to purify themselves. [56] Then sought they for Jesus, and spake among themselves, as they stood in the temple, What think ye, that he will not come to the feast? [57] Now both the chief priests and the Pharisees had given a commandment, that, if any man knew where he were, he should shew it, that they might take him.*

What irony of life. The purifier was there amongst them, yet they had driven Him away. Jesus could purify. He had given Lazarus a new body. Four days rot was changed in a moment. The dead Lazarus heard the Master's call, yet the "living" could not.

God's plan for our deliverance started rolling with the raising of Lazarus. Caiaphas just did not know, as much as he said to the other scribes and Pharisees, all of them just did not know.

When Jesus neither comes nor gives a word, His will not worry; the resurrection miracle is worth waiting for, worth believing.

What was too late of the medical was time for the raising. Ours is a beautiful story in the making.

Storms will come. Death will come. Jesus gives a word for all situations, as He said to the disciples in **Matthew 14:27…..***Be of good cheer; it is I; be not afraid.*

Meanwhile, you and me, let us sing, like the Gaithers do:

Oh, they tell me of a home far beyond the skies
Oh, they tell me of a home far away
Oh, they tell me of a home where no storm clouds rise
Oh, they tell me of an unclouded day.

Oh, the land of cloudless day
Oh, the land of an unclouded sky
Oh. they tell me of a home where no storm clouds rise
Oh, they tell me of an unclouded day.

Oh, they tell me of a home where my friends have gone
Oh, they tell me of a land far away
Where the tree of life in eternal bloom
Sheds it's fragrance through the uncloudy day.

Psalms 89:34 *My covenant will I not break, nor alter the thing that is gone out of my lips.*

Oh, the land of cloudless day
Oh, the land of an unclouded sky
Oh. they tell me of a home where no storm clouds rise
Oh, they tell me of an unclouded day.

Oh, they tell me that He smiles on His children there
And His smile drives their sorrows away
And they tell me that no tears ever come again
In that lovely land of an uncloudy day.

Oh, the land of cloudless day
Oh, the land of an unclouded sky
Oh. they tell me of a home where no storm clouds rise
Oh, they tell me of an unclouded day...

https://www.letssingit.com/bill-and-gloria-gaither-and-their-homecoming-friends-lyrics-the-unclouded-day-rkrq2hp
LetsSingIt - The Internet Lyrics Database (accessed 07/01/2019)\

ALWAYS, it is about Jesus. It is about God, it is about Godliness, it is about the Holy Spirit of the Lord. This is phenomenal.

Any day the Lord raises His own, is an awesome day. The delay should not worry us, or concern us. We cannot fear, we cannot be burdened, we cannot be anxious. The delay is very deliberate.

No.

Chapter 8

Occupy Till I Come

Before Jesus was crucified, He told a telling parable.

The Bible says in **Luke 19: 11**....... *he added and spake a parable, because he was nigh to Jerusalem, and because they thought that the kingdom of God should immediately appear. He said therefore, A certain nobleman went into a far country to receive for himself a kingdom, and to return. [13] And he called his ten servants, and delivered them ten pounds, and said unto them, Occupy till I come.* **Luke 19:12**

To occupy is to inhabit, to lodge, to live, to dwell, to reside in, to conquer, to subjugate. This is a short but very loaded statement – **occupy till I come**.

Psalms **89:34** *My covenant will I not break, nor alter the thing that is gone out of my lips.*

Jesus was telling the parable so that there was no confusion. Everyone had to know, there was no date, but coming back was not in doubt. Everyone would also know, the story of salvation was a long haul assignment.

This assignment was going to involve 100% of the population. The Bible says the nobleman called his ten servants; it does not say the nobleman called ten servants, which would have meant some were left unassigned. He called his ten servants – all of them.

Luke 19:14 says *But his citizens hated him, and sent a message after him, saying, We will not have this man to reign over us.*

The servants were to occupy the land of the citizens. The citizens hated the nobleman; they did not want his rulership.

Jesus continued - *And it came to pass, that when he was returned, having received the kingdom, then he commanded these servants to be called unto him, to whom he had given the money, that he might know how much every man had gained by trading.* **Luke 19:15.**

The servants were not told how they were going to trade. One thing was sure; the servants were behind enemy lines. The citizens did not like the nobleman. It was a tough call.

The nobleman wanted to know how much each had gained by trading. Trading is exchange, dealing, swapping, and substitution – all for profit.

There was an assessment - how did you trade. The quantum, the numbers did not matter, what mattered was the percentage. It had to be 100%.

If all servants got a 100%, then all the citizens may or could have been converted. They may or could have loved the nobleman. The citizens may or could have benefited.

The nobleman was angry when the third sat on his talent because the nobleman could not get all the citizens on his side. The servants and the citizens were important to the nobleman.

Everyone wants to associate with 10/10 people or 20/20 vision people. The nobleman did too.

Schools of this world want fifteen pointers, or 20 pointers, they want 100% performance. These schools have awards, cream blazers.

This is what the nobleman also wanted; he had to give his "cream blazers" to his servants. Not anyhow, but there was a threshold.

The nobleman wanted his servants to walk with him. He was not short of people or servants. He did not want those that crossed his path, he wanted those that saw things the way he did, who talked the way he did, who lived the way he did.

Our nobleman, Jesus, also want 100% performance. He has a threshold, the Ten Commandments. That is a set of principles to live by. When its 100%, then it is a 10/10 association.

Grace we have received, abundant grace. We are already servants of the nobleman, and we eat at his table. We are chosen, we are called, and we are privileged to be associated with the nobleman. But that is not enough.

We need to walk in his shoes. Occupy; take charge, until he comes back!

As Christians, we are often happy with fractional performance. We respect our parents and we are happy. Respecting parents is good, but not good enough.

We do not steal and we do not covet. That is also good, but that will give us a 3/10.

We do not make for ourselves any graven images and we also remember the Sabbath day and pray to keep it holy, but that raises us to a 50% performance.

Brown blazers and cream blazers are not the same. It is not the colour, it is the identity.

The story continued [16] *Then came the first, saying, Lord, thy pound hath gained ten pounds.* [17] *And he said unto him, Well, thou good servant: because thou hast been faithful in a very little, have thou authority over ten cities. [18] And the second came, saying, Lord, thy pound hath gained five pounds. [19] And he said likewise to him, Be thou also over five cities.* **Luke 19**

Our 100% performance is not the real deal either. It is our attitude. When you have done well you know it. The first and second servants did not take long to meet the nobleman, they stood on the front line, and they sat on the front row.

ATTITUDE matters. Attitude separates people.

The first and second did not need to explain much. They simply stated *Lord, thy pound hath gained ten pounds.*

The reward was equally sure – you have been faithful. That was the reason for the reward. The nobleman added, faithful in a *very* little. Wow, that is huge.

Faithfulness brings authority as the reward. How you trade is a direct reflection of the authority that comes. The threshold is 20/20.

The nobleman says to everyone - to have authority, to have a stake in my kingdom, you have to walk the way I walk, eat the way I eat, and dress the way I dress. He says think, but the way I think. Live, but the way I live.

That is huge. We are not the nobleman, so how can we be like Him?

Psalms 89:34 *My covenant will I not break, nor alter the thing that is gone out of my lips.*

The third servant also ran. He did something. In **Luke 19: 20** the Bible says *And another came, saying, Lord, behold, here is thy pound, which I have kept laid up in a napkin:*

This servant was different. This servant does not talk about gain, he says, here is your pound. This servant says he laid up the pound in a napkin – really?

A napkin can be in the form of a paper towel, a serviette, a table cloth even. It can also be a rag or a duster.

This is who we are – the other servant. Our lives are soiled, we are fractional performers. We have a sense of Godliness, of the gospel, of the word of God, but deny its relevance, its power, on our lives.

The kingdom of God is not for the other servant, the one who is not even numbered.

This servant says in **Luke 19: 21** *For I feared thee, because thou art an austere man: thou takest up that thou layedst not down, and reapest that thou didst not sow.*

A nobleman is not your equal. It is good; it is very good that you are called. In fact it is excellent that the nobleman called you in the first place. The nobleman placed you at an advantage. You would otherwise have been part of the citizenry, but you were called. You are a chosen generation, but hey, your attitude can be that bad.

The Lord said to Moses, prepare against that day. Put your defences in place. The best defence is to be the 10/10 servant.

It is true the nobleman is austere. The nobleman is serious about his standards. He has a kingdom.

Jesus continues to tell the story, the parable. *²² And he (nobleman) saith unto him, Out of thine own mouth will I judge thee, thou wicked servant. Thou knewest that I was an austere man, taking up that I laid not down, and reaping that I did not sow: ²³ Wherefore then gavest not thou my money into the bank, that at my coming I might have required mine own with usury?* **Luke 19**

The nobleman just wanted common-sense living. The nobleman was asking for fair play – you got my pound, if you cannot use it, do the most logical thing – keep it safe and get a bank profit.

Banks do not do much. They have consistent rewards. You invest with them and you get a return.

Luke 19: 24 says *And he said unto them that stood by, Take from him the pound, and give it to him that hath ten pounds. ²⁵ (And they said unto him, Lord, he hath ten pounds.) ²⁶ For I say unto you, That unto every one which hath shall be given; and from him that hath not, even that he hath shall be taken away from him. ²⁷ But those mine enemies, which would not that I should reign*

Psalms 89:34 *My covenant will I not break, nor alter the thing that is gone out of my lips.*

over them, bring hither, and slay them before me. [28] *And when he had thus spoken, he went before, ascending up to Jerusalem.*

The not numbered servant was considered an enemy. An enemy combatant. One who is in your territory but is fighting against you. A definition of enemy combatant, edited by this author, taken from https://en.wikipedia.org/wiki/Enemy_combatant, says

This unnumbered servant was not only subject to capture and detention, but in addition, subject to trial and punishment by military tribunals. There is no mercy for enemy combatants. This servant got a chance to trade his position but he never did. It was time for judgement. It was time for justice.

This servant was the spy who secretly and without uniform passes the military lines of a belligerent in time of war, seeking to gather military information and communicate it to the enemy, or an enemy combatant who without uniform comes secretly through the lines for the purpose of waging war by destruction of life or property.

This servant was aggressive, argumentative, quarrelsome, and loud mouthed, this servant was confrontational. This servant was so combative he could be confrontational with the nobleman!

This servant was not entitled to the status of prisoners of war. He was an offender of the law of war, and thus subject to trial and punishment by military tribunals.

The nobleman was at war with the citizenry, and this not numbered servant should have known better. By his actions, he could not be numbered; he refused the nobleman's rulership over his life. He was simply, an enemy combatant.

Trading has conditions.

The first condition is in **Joshua 1:7-9**. The Bible says *[7] Only be thou strong and very courageous, that thou mayest observe to do according to all the law, which Moses my servant commanded thee: turn not from it to the right hand or to the left, that thou mayest prosper withersoever thou goest. [8] This book of the law shall not depart out of thy mouth; but thou shalt meditate therein day and night, that thou mayest observe to do according to all that is written therein: for then thou shalt make thy way prosperous, and then thou shalt have good success. [9] Have not I commanded thee? Be strong and of a good courage; be not afraid, neither be thou dismayed: for the LORD thy God is with thee whithersoever thou goest.*

A 100% pass rate is not playing marbles. It is hard and consistent work, it means ethical living, honest living, disciplined living, it means self-control, it means patience, it means faith, it means peace, it means love,

Psalms 89:34 *My covenant will I not break, nor alter the thing that is gone out of my lips.*

it means joy to serve, it means goodness and all. It means being fruitful.

It means faithfulness, to the letter and the spirit of Godliness. The fruit is distinct. There is no confusion; a banana and an apple are hugely different. All very good fruits but just so different. Yet we all need all.

High heaven is high heaven. Man cannot just fly into high heaven whilst outside the grade. Even the grace of Calvary cannot take everything into high heaven. Gravity will let go those that meet the standard of high heaven.

The eagles do not fly with the ducks. It simply does not happen.

Gravity is the biggest and most powerful force in the universe. It will not let go. Gravity is the biggest pull power God created. But Jesus has greater power.

The difference is, gravity pulls you down, it does not seek your consent. Jesus, more powerful as He is, will not force.

The second condition for 100% pass rate is **Psalms 1**. This is a powerful Psalm and needs no explanation or interpretation.

The Bible says; *1 Blessed is the man that walketh not in the counsel of the ungodly, nor standeth in the way of sinners, nor sitteth in the seat of the scornful.*

[2] *But his delight is in the law of the LORD; and in his law doth he meditate day and night.*

This is as straight as it can get.

The Bible says in **Malachi 3:3-18** the Lord will make sure the ducks just don't fly.

[3] *And he (God, The Holy Spirit, the Lord Jesus) shall sit as a refiner and purifier of silver: and **he shall purify** the sons of Levi, **and purge** them as gold and silver, **that they may offer unto the LORD an offering in righteousness.** [4] Then shall the offering of Judah and Jerusalem be pleasant unto the LORD, as in the days of old, and as in former years. [5] And **I will come near to you to judgment; and I will be a swift witness against** the sorcerers, and against the adulterers, and against false swearers, and against those that oppress the hireling in his wages, the widow, and the fatherless, and **that** turn aside the stranger from his right, and **fear not me, saith the LORD of hosts. [6] For I am the LORD, I change not;** therefore ye sons of Jacob are not consumed. [7] Even from the days of your fathers ye are gone away from mine ordinances, and have not kept them. Return unto me, and I will return unto you, saith the LORD of hosts. But ye said, Wherein shall we return? ....[13] Your words have been stout against me, saith the LORD. Yet ye say, What have we spoken so much against thee? [14] Ye have said, It is vain to serve God: and what profit is it that we have kept his ordinance, and*

that we have walked mournfully before the LORD of hosts? ...... ¹⁶ Then they that feared the LORD spake often one to another: and the LORD hearkened, and heard it, and a book of remembrance was written before him for them that feared the LORD, and that thought upon his name. ¹⁷ And they shall be mine, saith the LORD of hosts, in that day when I make up my jewels; and I will spare them, as a man spareth his own son that serveth him. ¹⁸ Then shall ye return, and discern between the righteous and the wicked, between him that serveth God and him that serveth him not.

There will always be a difference between those that worship God and those that know Him not. It will always be in what they possess, *love, joy, peace, longsuffering, gentleness, goodness, faith, ²³ Meekness, temperance* **Galatians 5:22-23**

In addition, the Bible says in **Psalms chapter 1**: **3** *And he shall be like a tree planted by the rivers of water, that bringeth forth his fruit in his season; his leaf also shall not wither; and whatsoever he doeth shall prosper. ⁴ The ungodly are not so: but are like the chaff which the wind driveth away. ⁵ Therefore the ungodly shall not stand in the judgment, nor sinners in the congregation of the righteous. ⁶ For the LORD knoweth the way of the righteous: but the way of the ungodly shall perish.*

This is significant. All rivers meet on Jane Island. But when one river dries, there is a risk that all will eventually dry out. What caused one to dry will cause the other to follow.

The good servants were faithful. They were the heroes of Hebrews 11. They were all in different situations and circumstances, but they had one thing in common – abiding trust in God.

They knew, the time does not matter, but one day, the nobleman WILL come back. That is faith.

The Bible says in **Hebrews 11:** *Now faith is the substance of things hoped for, the evidence of things not seen.....[3] Through faith we understand that the worlds were framed by the word of God, so that things which are seen were not made of things which do appear.*

This kind of faith, moves mountains. That kind of faith, speaks;

- Enoch had this testimony, that he pleased God,

- Sara judged him faithful, who had promised,

- Joseph, on his death bed, made mention of the departing of the children of Israel; and gave commandment concerning his bones,

- Moses saw and listened to an invisible God,

- The walls of Jericho fell down, after they were compassed about seven days.

Psalms 89:34 *My covenant will I not break, nor alter the thing that is gone out of my lips.*

There are times when what we see as temptations, are really tests. We are tested to see where we stand. Not because God does not know, but the testing of our faith works for our relationship with God, it creates in us a dependency upon God.

The Bible says in **Revelation 3: 10** *Because thou hast kept the word of my patience, I also will keep thee from the hour of temptation, which shall come upon all the world, to try them that dwell upon the earth.*

In **Genesis 22:1-5,** we read a story which seems so absurd, yet it is a story that speaks.

The Bible says in chapter **22** *And it came to pass after these things, that* **God did tempt Abraham,** *and said unto him, Abraham: and he said, Behold, here I am.* *² And he said, Take now thy son,* **thine only son** *Isaac,* **whom thou lovest,** *and get thee into the land of Moriah; and offer him there for a burnt offering upon one of the mountains which I will tell thee of. ³ And Abraham rose up early in the morning, and saddled his ass, and took two of his young men with him, and Isaac his son, and clave the wood for the burnt offering, and rose up, and went unto the place of which God had told him. ⁴ Then on the third day Abraham lifted up his eyes, and saw the place afar off. ⁵ And Abraham said unto his young men, Abide ye here with the ass; and I and the lad will go yonder and worship, and come again to you.*

Abraham knew the significance of the assignment. He knew he was going to Mount Moriah to worship and then **they** (him and the lad) would come back.

How we read, see and understand the instructions of God depends on our relationship. God did not give Abraham Isaac for slaughter. Isaac was a blessing. God's blessings do not come with tears.

Tears will come, because the liars and the accusers are with us; tears will flow, as long as the nobleman is not back yet. Trading will not be easy; there are crooks all over the place, enemy combatants. But the Lord will still bless. When the Lord has given the blessing, it remains a blessing, our God does not change.

It was not hard for Abraham to go to Mount Moriah; it was a three day's journey – so what? And

Jesus would be in the grave three days. It is just how God preferred it.

It is how we see; it is us, who do change. It is our faith, it is our attitude, it is our prayer, which does change.

In this Genesis story, the Bible is saying a profitable relationship with God ought to be personal. There are situations and circumstances that ought to tell us – this is personal. Walk on, and the Lord will do the rest.

Psalms 89:34 *My covenant will I not break, nor alter the thing that is gone out of my lips.*

Servants have their place and donkeys have their role. When children of God decide for a powerful relationship with their God, they ought to leave the servants where they should and the donkeys in their place.

Prayer is that type of relationship. Effective prayer, rewarding prayer, is personal prayer. Safe journeys prayers are prayers for all, servants and donkeys alike and together, but prayers for Godliness are private and personal.

Leave the servants and the donkeys behind. Fervent prayer is very personal. Abraham had been summoned by God to prayer at Mount Moriah, and a three day preparation against that day was important – Abraham walked until he had to leave the servants and the donkeys. Personal prayer is for sons and their father!

Our faith should be a pillar from which we can lean and magnify God. We cannot be careless about our faith.

Carelessness about our faith is often a result of the company we walk in. Abraham could not take the servants and the donkeys to the place of sacrifice. It was not for them. Abraham could not be careless about the things of God, and Godliness.

Paul says to the Corinthians, in **1 Corinthians 15:33** Bad company corrupts good morals.

Morals are the principles, the messages, the ethics, the standards and the meanings that we share and are credited to our lives. When we get careless with our faith, we are misunderstood and our lives do not mean what they are meant to mean.

The fourth trading condition is know who you are trading with. This is what the Bible says in John 10.

Who you follow, who you transact with, you ought to know. Strangers will take what is yours. – they will take your crown, your profit, your interest.

The Bible says in **John 10:4** .... *and the sheep follow him: for they know his voice. [5] And a stranger will they not follow, but will flee from him: for they know not the voice of strangers.*

The sheep know the voice of the shepherd.

Jesus says He came so that we could have life, *and that they might have it more abundantly.* **John 10:14** *I am the good shepherd, and know my sheep, and am known of mine. [15] As the Father knoweth me, even so know I the Father: and I lay down my life for the sheep.*

Paul would say to the Corinthians [18] *For the preaching of the cross is to them that perish foolishness; but unto us which are saved it is the power of God. [19] For it is written, I will destroy the wisdom of the wise, and will bring to nothing the understanding of the prudent.*

Psalms 89:34 *My covenant will I not break, nor alter the thing that is gone out of my lips.*

[20] Where is the wise? where is the scribe? where is the disputer of this world? hath not God made foolish the wisdom of this world? [21] For after that in the wisdom of God the world by wisdom knew not God, it pleased God by the foolishness of preaching to save them that believe. **1 Corinthians 1:18-21**

The not numbered servant was in dispute, with other servants and with the nobleman. He would not be quiet. He decided, if the nobleman will say, come now, let us reason together, or put your case forward, then he would be ok. But it was time out for reasoning, for putting his case forward. The servant had time, before the nobleman came, to reason.

The instructions were never vague. It was his attitude, not the instructions.

The nobleman gave authority. The servants were given rulership in the cities of the kingdom.

Jesus also does – eternal life.

Jesus promised *[28] And I give unto them eternal life; and they shall never perish, neither shall any man pluck them out of my hand. [29] My Father, which gave them me, is greater than all; and no man is able to pluck them out of my Father's hand. [30] I and my Father are one. [31] Then the Jews took up stones again to stone him.* **John 10**

The Bible does not tell how the nobleman came back, but he did.

Revelation 1:7 says *Behold, he (Jesus) cometh with clouds; and every eye shall see him, and they also which pierced him: and all kindreds of the earth shall wail because of him. Even so, Amen.*

Those who will go and those that will rise are those that DID the Lord's bidding.

TIME matters. Time always exposes the foolish.

The five of the ten virgins were exposed by time.

People have a problem handling delay. Most just get distracted by impure thoughts and bad habits. One preacher said, what you cannot conquer today will conquer you out of heaven.

When Moses delayed on Mt Sinai, the people built a calf for their god.

The Bible says in **2 Peter 3:9** *The Lord is not slack concerning his promise, as some men count slackness; but is longsuffering to us-ward, not willing that any should perish, but that all should come to repentance.*

God is not slack on fulfilling His promise. He has judged we are not ready. Jesus delay is our opportunity to return to the Father.

PREPAREDNESS matters. It defines who we are.

Psalms **89:34** *My covenant will I not break, nor alter the thing that is gone out of my lips.*

State of preparedness separates people. The state of preparedness is judged by how we come out of crisis situations:

Real character is seen in the hour of crisis. The difference between the wise and the foolish virgins came at midnight – when all was dark or bad. That character is not transferable, it is your identity, and it is personal.

Crisis creates an opportunity for us to turn back. Either to God or to destruction. Crisis situations, inadvertently, open doors.

In **Hebrews 11:13** the Bible says Enoch, Moses Sarah, Joseph and many more; *These all died in faith, not having received the promises, but having seen them afar off, and were persuaded of them, and embraced them, and confessed that they were strangers and pilgrims on the earth. [14] For they that say such things declare plainly that they seek a country. [15] And truly, if they had been mindful of that country from whence they came out, they might have had opportunity to have returned. [16] But now they desire a better country, that is, an heavenly: wherefore God is not ashamed to be called their God: for he hath prepared for them a city.*

What made these stand out, was because they were not mindful of what they had left behind. This means the opportunities to turn back came, but they were not tied up to yesterday, they were 20/20 on the future. They had made a commitment, to faithfully trade, as they waited for the nobleman.

Trading is never easy. **Hebrews 11:33** says all these servants *Who through faith subdued kingdoms, wrought righteousness, obtained promises, stopped the mouths of lions,* went through perilous times.

They had strength of purpose, they were on a mission, and the nobleman was coming back. In the process of trade, they *[34] Quenched the violence of fire, escaped the edge of the sword, out of weakness were made strong, waxed valiant in fight, turned to flight the armies of the aliens.*

Joseph's crisis was in Potiphar's house, and the Hebrew boys had a crisis on the plain of Dura.

Joseph, the Hebrew boys, the wise virgins, were prepared, regardless of the time.

We have an open door. The instructions were to trade, to bring a profit. The nobleman knows our works.

As we occupy, we are cognizant of the fact that challenges are proportionate. You will not get what you cannot bear.

The Bible says the word of God will build us up so that we are equal to the task. This word, as said by Paul to the Romans in **Romans 15:13,** *Now the God of hope fill*

Psalms 89:34 *My covenant will I not break, nor alter the thing that is gone out of my lips.*

you with all joy and peace in believing, that ye may abound in hope, through the power of the Holy Ghost.

The challenges are there, there is opportunity to go back. Even good man can fall. **Psalms 37:23-24** then says *[23] The steps of a good man are ordered by the LORD: and he delighteth in his way. [24] Though he fall, he shall not be utterly cast down: for the LORD upholdeth him with his hand.*

Hebrews 11:6 says *But without faith it is impossible to please him: for he that cometh to God must believe that he is, and that he is a rewarder of them that diligently seek him*

The Lord said, occupy till I come. In **Revelation 3:11** he says *Behold, I come quickly: hold that fast which thou hast, that no man take thy crown. [12] Him that overcometh will I make a pillar in the temple of my God, and he shall go no more out: and I will write upon him the name of my God, and the name of the city of my God, which is new Jerusalem, which cometh down out of heaven from my God: and I will write upon him my new name.*

Our ATTITUDE, TIME and PREPAREDNESS, will separate us. We will all have opportunity to turn back, but our FAITH will keep us focused on the coming King!

━━━ *Chapter 9* ━━━

A Cloud Of Witnesses

Sin is pleasureful, but that pleasure is for a season, a very short season.

The consequence of sin is death. Sin has no colour, it is not limited by geography, and sin is sin.

We cannot do Godly things our way. Whatever part of the path, hills or valleys, rivers or streams, there are witnesses. We are surrounded.

The Lord cares. The Lord will do awesome things for us. The Bible says in **Psalm 5:12,** *For thou, LORD, wilt bless the righteous; with favour wilt thou compass him as with a shield.*

Psalms 89:34 *My covenant will I not break, nor alter the thing that is gone out of my lips.*

The Lord knows the dangers we face every day, every moment. The Psalmist says the Lord will compass us with favour. Favour will be our shield; grace will keep us awake to the challenges. Grace will give us strength to walk the way and run the race.

An expression of our daily lives says favour is not fair. It is a true saying. Favour is benefit not deserved.

We do not deserve and neither could we even dream, that God, the Creator of the Universe, the Giver of Life, would come down for our deliverance, for our healing, for our peace.

This, our God, knows we need to be delivered, every single day, from the consequences of wilful sin and all the trials and temptations. We also need to be delivered, from the sin that we inherited, yes, that one, from the Garden of Eden.

It has to be favour. It can only be favour. Because sin is huge, so burdensome, so so heavy you cannot do anything. It needs Jesus, the burden bearer. There is no bishop, no deacon, no pastor, no elder, no one, who can carry their own sin, let alone the sin of another, or the sin of the congregation.

When Jesus has carried our sin burden, we then can sing. We can praise God.

Man, by nature, is not worthy to praise God. The angels are, but still God says He wants to inhabit the praises of

His people. This is favour. He is an awesome God. And there are witnesses all around us, to tell eternity that God favoured creation called man. The angels of God will be witnesses.

Our neighbours, our families, and strangers too, will all be witnesses. The word of God will be a witness and Jesus the Christ will be a witness. We are surrounded.

When Jesus fed the 5 000 people, it meant there were 5000 witnesses. The Bible says women were not counted, and neither were children, on that particular day.

This means there were more witnesses than the Bible recorded. This is a principle of life – there are always more witnesses than you think – to your works, to your words, to your steps, to your conversations.

Should we forget what the Lord would have said or done for us, there would be witnesses to remind us.

We cannot argue against their story. They were there, they saw, they touched, they felt and they heard.

.The disciples, when they faced the storm in the sea, they forgot Jesus had fed 5 000 a few hours earlier, and Jesus reminded them.
We cannot forget, we should never forget.

Psalms 89:34 *My covenant will I not break, nor alter the thing that is gone out of my lips.*

In the wilderness, the children of Israel drank sweet waters from a fountain that was bitter a few hours or even minutes earlier.

So bitter was the first experience and so sweet was the next, because the Lord was there. All the children of Israel were witnesses at Marah but a few days more in the wilderness they forgot they even had God as their God.

It is interesting that whilst we focus on the bitterness of the waters at Marah, the others focus on the sweetness, the joy and the laughter that came out at Marah. The witnesses tell us, remind us, of the grace we have received, the privileges of peace and joy that come from just knowing God.

We have witnesses. How bitter we think the waters are is really an attitude issue. The Moslems chose to celebrate the joy and laughter at Marah. What we think and how we view the things of God is a function of our attitude – it is a reflection of what we focus on – the good or the bad.

There are witnesses, people who can testify whether or not we should be crying and complaining, or singing, joyful and praising. Those people may just be citizens, not servants. Those are the people in our daily lives.

The witnesses may be the people we are yoked to. Who we yoke ourselves with is very important. Who we yoke ourselves to may be just the person who determines the outcome of what we do, for God or against God.

The Bible relates a story in **2 Chronicles 20:35-37** when Jehoshaphat king of Judah joined himself with Ahaziah king of Israel, who was known to do wicked things.

We have alluded to the fact that Jesus said occupy till I come, and that what we do is one thing – we trade. This king decided to join himself with Ahaziah to make ships to go to Tarshish.

By all interpretation, this seems quite noble and good. What could be so wrong with making ships, the route is there and the demand is there?

But God was not pleased. The Bible says in verse 37, *Then Eliezer the son of Dodavah of Mareshah prophesied against Jehoshaphat, saying, because thou hast joined thyself with Ahaziah, the LORD hath broken thy works. And the ships were broken, that they were not able to go to Tarshish.* **2 Chronicles 20**

The Lord will break our works if we are not mindful about who we get tied up to. Even in everyday language, the saying goes, birds of a feather flock together. And the Bible says no two people can walk together unless they agree.

There are witnesses, we just need to be careful, circumspect and alert, the Bible calls it.

Psalms 89:34 *My covenant will I not break, nor alter the thing that is gone out of my lips.*

Hebrews 12: 1 says *Wherefore seeing we also are compassed about with so great a cloud of witnesses, let us lay aside every weight, and the sin which doth so easily beset us, and let us run with patience the race that is set before us,* **²** ***Looking unto Jesus the author and finisher of our faith; who for the joy that was set before him endured the cross, despising the shame, and is set down at the right hand of the throne of God.*** **³** *For consider him that endured such contradiction of sinners against himself, lest ye be wearied and faint in your minds.*

The whole of Babylon was a witness, God's boys do not do funny things, they worship God, in truth and in spirit.

At Shushan the palace, in Esther's time, there were witnesses, one hundred and twenty princes and all their kingdoms, God's girls do not do funny things either, they take charge, quietly but effectively.

After the Mt Camel experience, Jezebel was a witness, God's men are powerful. They "flock" with God. Even when Elijah ran hundreds of miles from Jezebel, God had a plan for His man.

The common thread in all these people, they prayed. In **Jeremiah 33:3** the Lord says *Call unto me, and I will answer thee, and show thee great and mighty things, which thou knowest not.*

And

Isaiah 29:13-15 says *Wherefore the Lord said, Forasmuch as this people draw near me with their mouth, and with their lips do honour me, but have removed their heart far from me, and their fear toward me is taught by the precept of men: ....[15]* **Woe unto them that seek deep to hide their counsel from the LORD, and their works are in the dark, and they say, Who seeth us? and who knoweth us?**

Careful, careful. Our God is an all seeing God, an all knowing God, and an Omni-present God.

Chapter 10

Pray & Prepare

The biggest threat to our existence as Christians is compromise. We are so into this world we hardly care what image we reflect.

David says in **Psalms 51: 12** *Restore unto me the joy of thy salvation; and uphold me with thy free spirit.* [13] *Then will I teach transgressors thy ways; and sinners shall be converted unto thee.*

The world is playing its music, and it is good music to our ears. We need the Spirit of the Lord to sustain us, in the spiritual. The music the world plays is very loud, and it is well dressed. There is a risk we may start dancing the way the bad guys do. The music the world plays is not for God. It is that simple.

Prayer makes us aware of the music of compromise. We cannot afford to compromise our positions in Christ. As the saying goes, what we get by compromise, we will also keep by compromise.

The Bible talks about Cain. Cain was brought up in a family that knew God, yes they no longer had access to some of the benefits of Eden, but they were still in the presence of God.

Cain knew what he had to do and when. Instead Cain, decides to do it differently, in plain view of God. This is also what we do, regardless of the instructions.

This is the tragedy of Cain. God's instructions are plain and simple. But we have a way of disobeying God. We are not saying Lord we will not worship you; we are saying we will just do it in a different way.

With God, that will not do. One preacher said we will go to heaven the old fashioned way.

We cannot be confused; cabbages and sheep are totally different. We are living in a toxic world that is so out of touch with Godliness. We believe we can substitute cauliflower for sheep!

Such is the foolishness of human beings when they walk, stand and seat where there is no God. Abel chose not to die for the foolishness of Cain, though it was Cain that actually killed Abel.

Psalms 89:34 *My covenant will I not break, nor alter the thing that is gone out of my lips.*

Abel was not going to follow big brother. We ought to be keenly aware that we cannot die for the foolishness of others. It does not matter how close these are to us.

We will choose Jesus, because He is the Son of God, and because He conquered sin. His sayings are true and we choose to believe Him. We do not believe the sayings, yes they are true, but we believe Him, the one who said. The Lord said. It is also that simple.

It does not matter how much technology we get, it does not matter how many times we fly to Mars or even live on the moon, The Lord will not change.

Who God was at creation is the same He is today and He will be the same to eternity.

It is only those who are led by the Spirit of God who are the children of God. Those that see us will be our judges. They will stand as witnesses, citizens or servants, but they will be the witnesses.

Tribulation does not exempt us from the standards that the word of God has set for us. Tribulation is only a chisel God uses to polish us.

Whatever tribulation one faces, that has happened to someone before. So tribulation does not account for much. It is really neither here nor there. We only need to get covered, fully covered, completely covered, when tribulation comes. Jesus, is our insurance.

The Bible says in **Romans 5:3-5** *And not only so, but we glory in tribulations also: knowing that tribulation worketh patience; [4] And patience, experience; and experience, hope: [5] And hope maketh not ashamed; because the love of God is shed abroad in our hearts by the Holy Ghost which is given unto us.*

For emphasis, the Bible also says in **1 Peter 5:8** *Be sober, be vigilant; because your adversary the devil, as a roaring lion, walketh about, seeking whom he may devour: [9] Whom resist stedfast in the faith, knowing that the same afflictions are accomplished in your brethren that are in the world. [10] But the God of all grace, who hath called us unto his eternal glory by Christ Jesus, after that ye have suffered a while, make you perfect, stablish, strengthen, settle you.*

This is a fact of life. We cannot run away from it, but we can stand, fight and conquer.

Paul to the Ephesians says *[15] See then that ye walk circumspectly, not as fools, but as wise, [16] Redeeming the time, because the days are evil. [17] Wherefore be ye not unwise, but understanding what the will of the Lord is. [18] And be not drunk with wine, wherein is excess; but be filled with the Spirit; [19] Speaking to yourselves in psalms and hymns and spiritual songs, singing and making melody in your heart to the Lord; [20] Giving thanks always for all things unto God and the Father in the name of our Lord Jesus Christ;* **Ephesians 5**

Psalms 89:34 *My covenant will I not break, nor alter the thing that is gone out of my lips.*

It is tough and the tougher keep going. Heaven is not for the faint hearted. That is why the Bible says faint not. In **Galatians 6:9** the Bible says *And let us not be weary in well doing: for in due season we shall reap, if we faint not.*

When strength is gone, we ought to remember the Lord answers prayer. Pray and plead - the Lord restore, Lord heal, Lord raise!

As the Bible says in **Isaiah 40: 28** *Hast thou not known? hast thou not heard, that the everlasting God, the LORD, the Creator of the ends of the earth, fainteth not, neither is weary? there is no searching of his understanding. [29] He giveth power to the faint; and to them that have no might he increaseth strength. [30] Even the youths shall faint and be weary, and the young men shall utterly fall: [31] But they that wait upon the LORD shall renew their strength; they shall mount up with wings as eagles; they shall run, and not be weary; and they shall walk, and not faint.*

We should overcome mountains of challenges and adversity. We feel so ok and even comfortable in the territory of the enemy. We need to pray for strength to move away, away from anything that slips. We cannot afford any slip-ups, blunders, errors, omissions. We cannot afford mistakes.

David says in **Psalm 119:11** *Thy word have I hid in mine heart, that I might not sin against thee.*

We should not hide from the word of God, we should hide it in our hearts, make this word very personal, cherish the word, love the word, keep the word.

If we lose the word, we have lost the fight. It is the ammunition. It is the heat seeking missile. We say the word, and we live the word, and we are home.

God will show us what we ought to see. In this journey, whilst we wait for our God, to physically take us home, it is not everything that we should open our eyes to. Our senses betray us, the passions, the desires, the feelings, all fail us.

Regardless of what we come across, we need to keep walking, there is light at the end of the tunnel. Jesus is coming back.

We need to saturate ourselves with Godly things. There is just no other way.

The challenges will be different. Different challenges to different people. But the challenges are proportionate, that is what the Bible says ... and even soldiers have ranks.

1 Corinthians 10:13 says *There hath no temptation taken you but such as is common to man: but God is faithful, who will not suffer you to be tempted above that ye are able; but will with the temptation also make a way to escape, that ye may be able to bear it.*

Psalms 89:34 *My covenant will I not break, nor alter the thing that is gone out of my lips.*

The temptation ALWAYS comes with the way of escape. Prayer will show us the way. God gives wisdom to know what, how and when.

And the victory is never our own. Victory belongs to God. Solomon says in **Proverbs 21:31** *The horse is prepared against the day of battle: but safety is of the LORD.*

The ladies of **Mark 16:1-4** asked who would roll the stone away.

They were thinking about a stone that they had seen three days earlier. Our God loves us that much, before we get there, the stone is rolled away.

We may not see it, we may not feel it, but we ought to believe it, and walk on.

This stone was rolled away not because it was ordinary; it was rolled away before they got there because it was a very great stone. The Bible says in **Mark 16:4** *And when they looked, they saw that the stone was rolled away: for it was very great.*

The Lord knows what we can roll away and what He needs to roll away.

This is God. The stones God will roll will not always be the same, and it will not be one stone. Over your lifetime, the stones will be so many you lose count, but they have all been rolled away.

The stones will be different, by weight, by type and by volume. Even a heap of small stones God will wheel away.

Whatever we come across, we should take it in our stride, because we have great hope. The Bible says while we walk, we are looking, not to man, not to circumstance, but we are *Looking for that blessed hope, and the glorious appearing of the great God and our Saviour Jesus Christ;* **Titus 2:13**

Justified, sanctified, we can only wait and hope for glorification – the Lord is faithful. Glory is the end game.

With that mind set, we are sure, we know, that whatever is challenging us now will pass. We are not encumbered by the finite and the mortal.

We prepare for the unavoidable. The avoidable we can see, we have control over, and we have God given power to choose right.

Bad friends are avoidable. Success demands that one is very conscious of their influence. These are not all weather friends. They are friends when you have a common something. That thing which pulls you together, yet they are not for heaven. You need stamina to resist friendly fire. Even friendly fire can kill.

Psalms 89:34 *My covenant will I not break, nor alter the thing that is gone out of my lips.*

Friends agree, as much as in marriage, boys and girls agree, then lobola is paid. Employment also means there is an agreement, there is an understanding, there is common purpose. God wants the same.

Broken walls are avoidable. You cannot lean on a broken wall. It will go down with you. We simply do not trust broken walls or trust mortal beings. You cannot fix broken walls. The best you can do is take them to God in prayer. The Lord can fix broken walls – not you, not me!

The proud are avoidable. The scornful are avoidable. Those who will just want to pull you down are avoidable. These will be there. Those who will want to take your crown. We all need to watch out for those that demean what we do. These will not only discourage, but they will also trick and trap.

The enemy always wants to remove you from the high ground. The Lord, the Bible says, has made us beacons of light, but the enemy wants to stifle our flame.

The easiest weapon the enemy employs is letting God's children get involved in cheap conversations. The tongue is a sure fire source. The fire, once started, will not be extinguished until the forest is gone. Even green trees will burn.

Whatever situation we find ourselves in, captivity will end. Jesus will deliver, because He is coming back. The time does not matter. We just keep in position. Jesus knows the co-ordinates of where we stand, where we sit, where we lie down, dead or alive.

Always, the way we look at life depends on the window through which we are looking. Tainted by sin, all we see is sin and its consequences, but hey, there are still Godly people out there. If the colour of sin is blue, then all we are seeing is blue, but hold on, there is a white in the midst of the blue, or the red or the yellow.

And that exceptional colour, that white in the middle of the blue, or the red or the yellow, that white, should never be blurred or smudged; it should be as neat as they come – the justified and the sanctified. Waiting for glorification, for eternity!

Jesus says in **John 14:8-9**. He who has seen me has seen the father, after Philip had asked. The Bible says *Philip saith unto him, Lord, show us the Father, and it sufficeth us. ⁹ Jesus saith unto him, Have I been so long time with you, and yet hast thou not known me, Philip? he that hath seen me hath seen the Father; and how sayest thou then, Show us the Father?*

We have seen the Christ, we have seen what He does, He has touched us, and He has shown us the way to the Father. We cannot lose the way of the cross, the way to the Father; it is marked – by the blood of Jesus.

Psalms 89:34 *My covenant will I not break, nor alter the thing that is gone out of my lips.*

Where everything is smooth sailing, no waves no storm, man will not pray. Adversity reminds us that there is God.

Our stories will be different, and your story could be the way to glorifying God, just as much as the death of Lazarus was.

When we live life, we cannot seek to be understood. Some will understand life under God, some will not. As we wait upon the Lord, we ought to always remember that it is not the majority that determines Godliness, it is God who does. God's work is not by majority vote.

The Bible says in **Romans 3:11** *There is none that understandeth, there is none that seeketh after God.*

It is favour; it is grace, to know God, and the power of His presence. In captivity, we also pray. We do not raise up our hands in surrender, we raise up our hands in praise.

Even children of God get "captured". Captivity is not good. We can be captured by poverty, by disease, by hurt, by disability, by death of the people we love and look up to. It does not matter the name, it is still captivity and it is not good.

Fear too, can capture people of God. Jabez, an honourable man, prayed. He says keep me from evil. It is true; there is a lot of evil out there.

The Bible says in **1 Chronicles 4:10-11**, *And Jabez called on the God of Israel, saying, Oh that thou wouldest bless me indeed, and enlarge my coast, and that thine hand might be with me, and that thou wouldest keep me from evil, that it may not grieve me! And God granted him that which he requested.*

I want to believe that this was not a good time. All things were not going well. All these issues Jabez prayed for, affect every single one of us. The difference is in the magnitude, the significance of each in our relative lives.

We are as different inside as we are outside. We see things differently, even when it is exactly the same things. And we respond differently to these situations.

What then shape our responses is our character, our mind, how we have prepared, how we have prayed and how we pray.

Christianity is very intentional. After we have told our story, or another has told our story, the judgement, the verdict should be, these people stay in the presence of the Lord. Even our children should say the same – we walk the paths our parents, our grandparents, our teacher, our pastor, our elder walks, because it is the path Jesus walked.

We cannot do any other, because this Jesus said that He is the way, He is the only way.

Psalms 89:34 *My covenant will I not break, nor alter the thing that is gone out of my lips.*

In everything, there is always a context, a community, a crisis point, a conflict of sorts, a cause and a culture. Children of God need to be the change agent – for the glory of God.

Regardless of how much we pray, when the Lord demands that we go to Ninevah, a Tashish always crops up. We should be vigilant, sin is costly. The devil presents an opportunity to turn back. God does too. He always gives an opportunity to turn back to Him, to trust Him, to believe Him. Who we follow is our choice. The choice is our prerogative. Choice is our priviledge, our right, our entitlement.

We are here because God is a merciful God. God does everything, so that we are so aware of His presence, even of His love. To Jonah He sent the wind and the fish. Only God knows what He will send, to keep our faith and our hope alive, in Him.

We run in various ways, but God will catch us somewhere, somehow. We cannot wait for the fish or the wind, because by the time we realize where we are and what is happening, someone, somewhere, has lost it all.

People should not regret that they gave us shelter, or food, or clothing, or a job. Jonah was a burden to the ship that was going to Tarshish.

Height should not be an issue, if you are not seeing right, then go on to higher ground, climb a tree if you will, so you are not a burden to other people. Zacchaeus did.

Our tree, our higher ground, our rock, is Jesus. Jesus is the source and meaning of life.

Peter says in **1 Peter 4:7** *But the end of all things is at hand: be ye therefore sober, and watch unto prayer.*

Being sober is a very good thing. You can think and you are logical. Peter says, being logical is not enough, pray. Whatever you thought about, pray about it.

The prophet Ezekiel then says in **Ezekiel 18:31,** *Cast away from you all your transgressions, whereby ye have transgressed; and make you a new heart and a new spirit: for why will ye die, O house of Israel?*

Ezekiel is actually puzzled, he sees what the Lord has done for Israel, but they are so obstinate. They are unmoved, stubborn, determined, fixed, and inflexible.

Jeremiah then says in **32:27**, the Lord says *Behold, I am the LORD, the God of all flesh: is there anything too hard for me?*

God is saying, even in your state, I can turn you around.

You do not need to work hard, pray. Christianity is more than the management of things God gave us, the talents,

---

Psalms 89:34 *My covenant will I not break, nor alter the thing that is gone out of my lips.*

the time, the wealth; it is the refusal to let things manage us.

Luke says in **12:15** *A man's life is not in the abundance of his possessions.*

It is these possessions that stop us from watching as we should, from praying as we should, from preparing as we should. It is these possessions that give us a bad attitude, an I am good to go attitude.

When the Bible says, as in this verse, of **Luke 12:15,** *Take heed, and beware of covetousness: for a man's life consisteth not in the abundance of the things which he possesseth.*

Jesus is imploring – listen, listen, listen. Things, these things called things, will take our attention from the Lord who created.

These things will want to make us believe we are lords. Lords of the flies? Perhaps, but no more.

Before God, we cannot stand.

The Lord says in **Acts 17:30** *And the times of this ignorance God winked at; but now commandeth all men everywhere to repent:*

And He says in **Isaiah 1:18** *Come now, and let us reason together, saith the LORD: though your sins be as scarlet,* *they shall be as white as snow; though they be red like crimson, they shall be as wool.*

Now we know, even the commandments we know. Jesus then says in **John 14:15** *If ye love me, keep my commandments.*

This is all there is, the nature of God is there for us to follow, not in two tablets of stone, not in the hands of Moses, not in the ark the priests carried, but in our hearts, built into even our conscience.

We are engraved in the palms of our Lord; we can do better than we do now. The Lord says in

Isaiah 49:15-16 *Can a woman forget her sucking child, that she should not have compassion on the son of her womb? yea, they may forget, yet will I not forget thee.* [16] ***Behold, I have graven thee upon the palms of my hands; thy walls are continually before me.***

Passionate, fervent prayer and fearless faith will keep us on track. Watch and pray, He said.

Your enemy, my enemy is seeking whom he may devour. The Bible says *Be sober, be vigilant; because your adversary the devil, as a roaring lion, walketh about, seeking whom he may devour:* **1 Peter 5:8**

An enemy is not a friend.

Psalms 89:34 *My covenant will I not break, nor alter the thing that is gone out of my lips.*

Esau lost a birth right to Jacob. Esau never saw it coming. Jacob was his brother.

We ought to be very alert, careful of those sitting in OUR tent – they have capacity to take our birth right.

As David would write, there are some who will literally push you over the edge. Watch and pray. David says in this verse **Psalm 118:13** *Thou hast thrust sore at me that I might fall: but the* LORD *helped me.*

Thank God David had prayed in Psalms 91, hide me oh God, and God did.

You cannot watch, you cannot pray, you cannot prepare if you are out of touch with your God, with Jesus, and the Holy Spirit of the Lord. Keep the kingdom connection alive, keep tagging at the rope, that red rope, Jesus is coming back.

The attire speaks. What you wear tells who you are. Joshua saw the "man" who then introduced himself as the commander of the host of heaven by what he wore. Put on the whole armour of God.

We cannot get swallowed up by what others are doing. We ought to stand. We cannot walk on other people's paths; we walk our paths, with Jesus, the Great Contender.

When we do, we are assured; the Lord will never leave us nor forsake us. Even the waves and the wind obey our God, His Holy Spirit and our Lord Jesus Christ.

Christians are selective – from friends to food. That is watching, that is preparing. Selective is being careful, it is discerning. Watching is making sure all the holes are plugged, closed. Only Jesus can plug the holes for us. We cannot allow our faith, our confidence in Christ, to seep out.

We have the commandments, and we have the testimony – so walk on soldier. **Revelation 7:14**

The Bible says in **Psalms 50:3** *Our God shall come, and shall not keep silence: a fire shall devour before him, and it shall be very tempestuous round about him.*

As John would say in **Revelation 3:20** *Behold, I stand at the door, and knock: if any man hear my voice, and open the door, I will come in to him, and will sup with him, and he with me.*

Jesus is at the door, and He is knocking. The purpose, He wants you, He wants me, on His table together with the great great multitude. **Revelation 7:9**

I cannot miss to be in that number, that multitude John saw, because God, the Lord Almighty, the Creator of the Universe, the Giver of Life, IS my God too. Jesus,

Psalms 89:34 *My covenant will I not break, nor alter the thing that is gone out of my lips.*

amazing Jesus, is my Saviour too; He is my friend, my way, my truth, my life. I believe Him, I trust Him, I love Him.

━━━━ *Chapter 11* ━━━━

Great Contender

From **Joshua 5:13-15**, it is apparent that Heaven has its commanders.

The Bible says *And it came to pass, when all the kings of the Amorites, which were on the side of Jordan westward, and all the kings of the Canaanites, which were by the sea, heard that the LORD had dried up the waters of Jordan from before the children of Israel, until we were passed over, that their heart melted, neither was there spirit in them anymore, because of the children of Israel.* **Joshua 5:1**

The thinking and the question was, which God could tame the waters of the Jordan. Dagon could not, Moloch could not, Baal could not and so on and so on.

Psalms **89:34** *My covenant will I not break, nor alter the thing that is gone out of my lips.*

Who was this God and who were these people?

They also remembered, years earlier, more than fourty years earlier, the same God had dried the waters of the red sea.

They remembered, these people had encamped where there was no fresh water, but their God had sweetened the waters of Marah.

Then they remembered they had heard some bread called manna had dropped from heaven to feed these people, and that the wind had brought birds called quails so that these people could feed in the desert.

Who was their God, and what were His plans across the Jordan. These kings were unease, they knew something was brewing. Could these people, and their God, mean well?

The Bible says in **Joshua 5:13-15** *And it came to pass, when Joshua was by Jericho, that he lifted up his eyes and looked, and, behold, there stood a man over against him with his sword drawn in his hand: and Joshua went unto him, and said unto him, Art thou for us, or for our adversaries? [14] And he said, Nay; but as captain of the host of the LORD am I now come. And Joshua fell on his face to the earth, and did worship, and said unto him, What saith my Lord unto his servant? [15] And the captain of the LORD's host said unto Joshua, Loose thy shoe from off thy foot; for the place whereon thou standest is holy. And Joshua did so.*

In the first chapter of Joshua, the Lord says to Joshua, be strong and of good courage. Joshua knew if he had had to take the cities, the towns and the lands of Canaan, he really needed all the assurance of heaven.

And heaven did not fail him.

God was in charge, it was His war, yet He says to Joshua be strong and of good courage. So what did this mean?

Who was Joshua in this "drama" and who was this man Joshua saw? At the battle between Goliath and David, this question was asked. Who are you?

The man Joshua saw said he was the commander of the host of the Lord. Yes, he was commander of the armies of heaven.

Joshua would never know, that Daniel would see this commander. Daniel had prayed, and no answers seemed to come, for twenty one days. The clouds then cleared, the darkness subsided, light came in, when the commander arrived. The Bible says in **Daniel 10:13**, *But the prince of the kingdom of Persia withstood me one and twenty days: but, lo, Michael, one of the chief princes, came to help me; and I remained there with the kings of Persia.*

Is it possible that the same that came down for Joshua is the same that came down for Daniel?

Psalms 89:34 *My covenant will I not break, nor alter the thing that is gone out of my lips.*

Daniel 12:1 then says *And at that time shall Michael stand up, the great prince which standeth for the children of thy people: and there shall be a time of trouble, such as never was since there was a nation even to that same time: and at that time thy people shall be delivered, every one that shall be found written in the book.*

Did Joshua see this Michael? Perhaps.

And the book of **Revelation,** in verse **5:5** says *And one of the elders saith unto me, Weep not: behold, the Lion of the tribe of Judah, the Root of David, hath prevailed to open the book, and to loose the seven seals thereof.*

I love this Michael, this Lion of the tribe of Judah, this commander of the armies of heaven. He means everything to me.

This Michael, I want to believe, is He that will come to take us home. He is the commander, He is Michael, He is Jesus, and He is the Son of God.

He has fought the Canaanites, He has fought the kings of Persia and all their princes, He has opened the books that nobody else could, He is Lord.

Michael, He who is like God or He who is what God is, is Lord of our lives. He is the Great Contender.

The Lordship of this Michael is not in doubt, He commands the host of heaven. He will be to us, as we would, that He is to us.

He will be Lord, if we choose Him to be Lord; He will be our adversary if we also choose Him to be.

This is Jesus the Christ. He is the basis of all Christian wars. In fact - all wars.

He wants us to prove our loyalty. He says to Joshua, I am not on your side, but I fight for all who fear the Lord. Even Joshua had to acknowledge, this "man" was bigger than him, so Joshua worshipped Him.

The challenge is with us, we fail to see who we ought to kneel down to. We have mixed allegiances. Today we belong to this side and tomorrow we are there.

Joshua just saw this "man" but this "man" had a whole army of heaven behind Him.

If this commander will fight for us, we ought to be on the side of the host of heaven. **Nahum 1:7** says *The LORD is good, a strong hold in the day of trouble; and he knoweth them that trust in him.*

Crossing over the Jordan and taking over was not going to be easy.

Psalms **89:34** *My covenant will I not break, nor alter the thing that is gone out of my lips.*

Just to cross the Jordan God had given an instruction, keep a space between the ark of God and the people, because you have not gone this way before.

Each day we walk the paths of this world, we need God to go before us, the Great Contender, so that he fights and finishes the battles before we get there.

Even the children of Israel had to prove their loyalty on the way. It is not all who left Egypt who got to Canaan. In fact, only two did.

We also prove our loyalty on this way, and not all of us will get there. Not all of us will get to heaven.

Jesus will take us where He has been. He was in heaven, came to earth, went back to heaven, and He is coming back.

Jesus will carry us through where and what He has passed through. He has been there, He has been in our situations, He has been in our time, He has been on our places, and He is in Heaven. He will take us there.

This Jesus knew and knows where His strength, His power, comes from. It comes from the Father.

Jesus prayed with the multitude, He also prayed with the few, and He prayed alone.

There is nothing that beats prayer. It is a statement of allegiance, it signifies where your loyalties are.

Elisha knew, if he was going to make a difference in the life of the family, he had to raise the dead boy. But hey, Elisha had to pray alone, with the dead boy.

It was a great contention – death and life are not friends.

Dead situations, dead prospects, dead everything always contends with the living.

In marriages there is contention, at school there is contention, at church there is contention, on the highways there is contention. Everywhere, there is contention, only God can make peace, can declare a cease fire, an armistice.

David says, I would have fainted, if I had not believed, that I would see the goodness of the Lord in the land of the living.

The Lord gives life. He contends for us. Contending is quite a mouthful of meaning. It is competing, it is opposing, challenging, struggling and resisting.

This is what the Lord does for us and in us. God challenges the enemy for control of our minds, for change of our behaviours.

The Bible says in **Isaiah 49:24-25** *Shall the prey be taken from the mighty, or the lawful captive delivered? ²⁵ But thus saith the LORD, Even the captives of the*

***Psalms* 89:34** *My covenant will I not break, nor alter the thing that is gone out of my lips.*

mighty shall be taken away, and the prey of the terrible shall be delivered: for I will contend with him that contendeth with thee, and I will save thy children.

Jesus sets free, even the captives of the mighty. The Lord will contend with them that contend with us. He will save our children too.

Hebrews tells us, we cannot throw away our confidence. The Bible says *Cast not away therefore your confidence, which hath great recompense of reward.* **Hebrews 10:35**

We have great reward, when the Lord God contends with our enemies, with anything that challenges our crown. Our minds, our senses, our environments, our everything. There is a higher reward.

There is compensation, reparations, settlement for all the trials and tribulations, if only we stand for God. The challenges may be private or public, either way; our loyalties ought to be clear.

It is not in vain that we worship God. For clarity, this definition of reparations is good. **War reparations** are payments made after a war by the vanquished to the victors.

They are intended to cover damage or injury inflicted during a war. Generally, the term *war reparations* refer to money or goods changing hands, but not to the annexation of land.

This is what we know. Of the wars that have been fought on this planet. War reparations have been paid; nations and peoples have been compensated. The principle is the same. The concept is, the victors ought to be rewarded.

I will take this further, based on historical records.

Making the defeated party pay a war indemnity is a common practice with a long history. In Ancient history, the imposition of reparations on a defeated enemy was often the beginning of forcing that enemy to pay a regular tribute.

The last instalment of the reparations German paid after World War I were only completed on *3 October 2010. The Germans had to take loans to pay off the war indemnities!*

Germany paid in forced labour, in United States dollars, in technology transfers, in manufacturing plant and equipment. Germany paid in cash and kind.

According to Article 14 of the Treaty of Peace with Japan (1951): "Japan should pay reparations to the Allied Powers for the damage and suffering caused by it during the war. Japan will promptly enter into negotiations with Allied Powers". .... Payments of reparations started in 1955, lasted for 23 years and ended in 1977.

Psalms 89:34 *My covenant will I not break, nor alter the thing that is gone out of my lips.*

After the Gulf War, Iraq accepted financial liability for damage caused in its invasion of Kuwait. Payments under this reparations program continue; as of July 2010. https://en.wikipedia.org/wiki/War_reparations

God will make sure, the enemy has paid. And God, will wipe away all tears.

The concept of reparations is from the word of God. This time, it will not be countries paying one to another, God will compensate. The battles belong to the Lord.

The Bible says in **Hebrews 10:37**, *For yet a little while, and he that shall come will come, and will not tarry.*

Arguably, the Bible is saying to us, hold on, it is not over until it is over.

It will only be over when Jesus, the Great Contender comes back, and He is coming back. The commander of the host of heaven whom Joshua saw had come to give Joshua courage. Joshua could not shrink back.

To Gideon God says the Midianites **will** come, but **I** will fight them. The enemy will fight me and you, because we were made in the image of God.

This means you and I, will need to do and should do what the children of God do.

David says in **Psalms 122:1** *I was glad when they said unto me, let us go to the house of God.*

This is the place where our armoury is housed, this is the place where strategy is mapped, this is the place where the war cry is read out and recited. This is the place of the gospel, the place of prayer, the house of the Lord, the house for all people.

The contention is very simple, yet so profound. Paul says in **1 Corinthians 1:18 – 20** *For the preaching of the cross is to them that perish foolishness; but unto us which are saved it is the power of God. ¹⁹ For it is written, I will destroy the wisdom of the wise, and will bring to nothing the understanding of the prudent. ²⁰ Where is the wise? where is the scribe? where is the disputer of this world? hath not God made foolish the wisdom of this world?*

The Lord is in it, and we will win it.

Our challenge is, we ought to be courageous, be as bold as Elijah. Elijah swore by the Lord before whom he stood. Elijah was so sure he stood before His God, He was never in doubt.

That kind of boldness comes when we know the Great Contender is on our side. The power of heaven was on show. God does not show off, but He shows up. And when He does show up, everything and everyone will know.

To Gehazi it took Elisha to pray for the Lord to show His presence on the hills surrounding Elisha. For His,

Psalms 89:34 *My covenant will I not break, nor alter the thing that is gone out of my lips.*

God will always show up. Those that know God, will know, He is always there, for me and for you.

As we continue in the presence of the Lord, the way Elijah did, it should be evident that each day we are stepping towards Zion's gates – the city of God.

One preacher said God threw the rain keys to Elijah. My imagination says God said to Elijah, you and me, can make Jezebel mad, and they sure did, Elijah and His God!

But Jezebel will not take it lying down, she will come back. But God is God.

God directs Elijah to go hide. Really? Hide from Jezebel? Yes, sure, God has His ways. He gives life. Life comes from God and not from the abundance of bread. Even sitting by a drying brook, Elijah got enough. Not in abundance, but enough.

If God trusts us to go to the brook; that is then where we belong. For a time, for a season.

He is the commander.

In this great contention, God reveals the Son to us. The Bible says *For God sent not his Son into the world to condemn the world; but that the world through him might be saved.* **John 3:17**

All this contention – the competing, the opposing, challenging, resisting and all, is God fighting our battles. This is favour.

The valleys, the tight spots, will be there, but the edges of life are with the Creator.

Christian life is not about doing good, it is about being good. Avoiding the anger, the bitterness, and the filth. That is what the word of God, in all its entirety, is struggling to achieve. Struggling, not because it has no power, but because men are choosing the way of the unGodly. And God does not force. Choice is privildge, even with and in God.

Paul in **Philippians 2:12** says *God gives the power to will and to do.* But this power He gives to those that want it. If you need it but do not want it, God will not force.

In this chapter the Bible says *Wherefore, my beloved, as ye have always obeyed, not as in my presence only, but now much more in my absence, work out your own salvation with fear and trembling.*

The Bible is saying, demonstrate that you are saved. Show where your loyalties lie.

These people obeyed when Paul was present, and Paul is urging them to do good even when he is absent. This

---

Psalms 89:34 *My covenant will I not break, nor alter the thing that is gone out of my lips.*

is all Paul could do. He would pray for them and encourage them, but the choice was theirs.

Paul goes on to say, on our own we cannot even choose right, but our sufficiency, the sufficiency of that power to choose right, is from God.

The Bible says in this **2 Corinthians 3:5** *Not that we are sufficient of ourselves to think anything as of ourselves; but our sufficiency is of God;*

What we do between the Godly and the ungodly is the choice.

Jude says in verse ²⁴ *Now unto him that is able to keep you from falling, and to present you faultless before the presence of his glory with exceeding joy.* The one Jude talks of is God. Only God can keep us from falling.

And Peter says in **1 Peter 1:16**. *Because it is written, Be ye holy; for I am holy.*

That is what Christianity is all about – we need to be holy, because Jesus, our Saviour, is Holy.

The Lord knows our works. We cannot hide, we cannot run. We are who we are, yet God gives opportunity to turn back to Him, to return.

This God, our God, is an equal opportunity God. He has numbered our days – so that none will say, I did not get a chance. It is by choice, to put our houses, our lives, in order.

Jesus will come to take those like him. Jesus will fly with those like Him, birds of a feather, flock together. The eagles cannot fly with the ducks. It is not good, and it is not possible!

Paul says to the Thessalonians, in **1 Thessalonians 4:16** *For the Lord himself shall descend from heaven with a shout, with the voice of the archangel, and with the trump of God: and the dead in Christ shall rise first:*

The angel of the Lord will record the co-ordinates of the graves of those that believe in this Great Contender. There will be no mistakes; you will not be left behind if you belong to the flock.

Those that are different will never know how the flock flies. It does not matter how close the graves are to each other, it does not matter even if it is a mass grave. It does not matter you or I, were lost at sea, it does not matter we were burnt beyond human recognition. Those of the feather know their language; they know where the other fell. They have their language, which is heard even in death.

Even if Jesus delays, as some would think it is delay, He will surely still come. This understanding I will illustrate by this example. I will call it the Boot Camp – United States Army.

Marine boot camp is extremely challenging – both physically and mentally. It is considered to be tougher

Psalms 89:34 *My covenant will I not break, nor alter the thing that is gone out of my lips.*

than the basic training programs of any of the other military services. All recruits go to one of two locations for basic training; Recruit Training Depot at Parris Island, South Carolina, or Recruit Training Depot at San Diego, California. Where recruits go depends largely upon where they enlist. Those who enlist west of the Mississippi will likely go through boot camp in San Diego, while those in the East will attend at Parris Island. There is only one boot camp to turn women into Marines -- Parris Island.

USMC Recruit Training
All Marine recruits start their training at the Marine Corps Recruit Depot (MCRD). This is where America's young men and women are transformed into Marines. Some believe that Marines are forged in a furnace of shared hardship and tough training. Shared, intense experience creates a bond so strong between Marines that nothing can stop them from accomplishing their mission.

Marine Corps recruits are trained not only physically and mentally, but morally as well. Forming the bedrock of any Marine's character are the Core Values -- Honour, Courage and Commitment. By incorporating these values into recruit training, a Marine is not just a basically trained, morally conscious Marine, but also a better American citizen who will return to society following his or her service to this country.

Taking Up The Challenge

Marines, both active and veterans, say that recruit training was the most difficult thing they ever had to do in their entire lives. It has to be that way to prepare young men and women to be part of the world's most elite fighting force.

Upon arrival at MCRD, a new recruit begins a three phase training program - a virtually non-stop journey - that results in the transformation from recruit to United States Marine.

Phase One - Week One Through Four

The first phase is the transition of civilian to recruit and it takes place at the MCRD, where recruits undergo strenuous physical training, martial arts and classes on such areas as Marine Corps history and first aid.

A recruit's first stop is called "Recruit Receiving". This is where recruits spend the first few days of their recruit training experience. This is where they receive their first haircut and initial gear issue, which includes items such as uniforms, toiletries and letter writing supplies. During this time they are also given full medical and dental screenings, and take the Initial Strength Test. This test consists of a one and a half mile run, sit-ups and pull-ups to test recruits to see if they're in shape to begin training. Recruits will also learn the Marine Corps values of honour, courage, and commitment. The rest of this phase is spent learning weapons handling from trained experts and completing the Confidence Course.

is gone out of my lips.

Phase Two – Week Five Through Nine

The second phase starts when recruits move up north to Edson Range, Weapons Field Training Battalion. hone their close combat skills and master Marksmanship Training. Every Marine is a rifleman first and foremost. It is during this time they will develop proficiency and confidence with their weapon. During this phase, they spend most of their time conducting field training and rifle qualifications. Recruits undergo gas chamber training, Field Firing Range and the Crucible event.

Phase Three – Week Ten Through Thirteen

For the third phase, recruits move back to the Depot where they undergo swim qualifications, a defensive driving course, testing of Marine Corps history, first aid, physical training, drill, and inspections and finally Family Day/Graduation.

The following are descriptions and details about some of the events listed above:-

The U.S. Marine Corps Core Values

The Corps' Core Values are Honour, Courage and Commitment. These values make up the bedrock of a Marine's character. During your training, you are taught these Core Values and the numerous others attached to them, such as integrity, discipline, teamwork, duty and esprit de Corps. Drill instructors, recruit training officers and Navy chaplains teach specific Core Values classes, but drill instructors also will talk one-on-one with you after other training events to see what values were learned and how you are affected. For example, a drill instructor might talk about overcoming fears after rappelling or not giving up after a long march.

Confidence Course

The Confidence Course is an 11-station obstacle course, which helps you build confidence as well as upper-body strength. You will tackle this course twice during your 13 weeks of training.

Physical Training

Physical Training, or "PT" as it is often called, comes in many forms. Recruit training uses a progressive physical training program, which builds up recruits to Marine Corps standards. Recruits will experience Table PT, a period of training in which a drill instructor leads several platoons through a series of demanding exercises while he demonstrates on a table. Recruits will also run, either individually or as a platoon or squad. Other PT consists of obstacle courses, circuit courses, or 3-, 5- or 10-mile conditioning marches.

Marksmanship Training

Marksmanship training teaches you the fundamentals of marksmanship with the M-16A2 service rifle. This training takes place over two weeks, the first of which is called "Snap-In Week". During this week, recruits are

Psalms **89:34** *My covenant will I not break, nor alter the thing that is gone out of my lips.*

introduced to the four shooting positions (standing, kneeling, sitting and prone) and a Primary Marksmanship Instructor shows how to fire, how to adjust rifle sights, how to take into account the effects of the weather, etc. Recruits also have the opportunity to fire on the Indoor Simulated Marksmanship Training machine. During the second week of marksmanship training, recruits fire a known-distance course with ranges of 200, 300 and 500 yards. Be prepared, rifle qualification will be on Friday.

Field Training
Field Training introduces you to field living and conditions. During the 3-day field training evolution, you will learn basic field skills from setting up a tent to field sanitation and camouflage. Also during the Field Training you get the opportunity to go through the gas chamber.

Field Firing Range (FFR)
FFR is a portion of training devoted to firing weapons in a field condition. During marksmanship training, you learn how to fire at a single target while in a stationary position. During FFR you learn how to fire at moving and multiple targets, while under low-light conditions and wearing your field protective (gas) mask.

Combat Water Survival
Combat Water Survival training develops your confidence in the water. All recruits must pass the minimum requirement level of Combat Water Survival-

4 (CWS-4), which requires recruits to perform a variety of water survival and swimming techniques. If recruits meet the CWS-4 requirements, you may upgrade to a higher level. All recruits train in the camouflage utility uniform, but if upgraded you may be required to train in full combat gear, which includes a rifle, helmet, flak jacket and pack.

Drill

Drill is the basic way in which platoons march and move from place to place. At first, you will practice by

just staying in step with the rest of the platoon and the drill instructor. During drill training, platoons will also compete in two drill competitions. Drill is mainly used to instill discipline, team pride and unit cohesion.

Family Day/Graduation

Family Day and Graduation take place on the last two days while on MCRD. Family Day occurs on Thursday and gives new Marines a chance to see their family and friends for the first time during on-base liberty. Graduation is conducted on Friday at the completion of the Transition Phase. It is a formal ceremony and parade, attended by family and friends and executed on the parade field.

The Crucible

The following is a description of the Marine Corps Crucible as told by the Marine Corps:

Psalms 89:34 My covenant will I not break, nor alter the thing that is gone out of my lips.

"We have two missions in the Marine Corps -- to win battles and make Marines," said Col. Bob Hayes, assistant deputy chief of staff for operations and training at the recruit depot here. "The Crucible is one piece of that effort."

The Crucible emphasizes trainee teamwork under stress. "Recruits get eight hours of sleep during the entire 54 hour exercise," said Sgt. Roger Summers, a Delta Company drill instructor in the 1st Recruit

Training Battalion at Parris Island. "They get two-and-a-half Meals Ready to Eat (MREs) and they are responsible for rationing out the food to themselves. Then we put them through tough physical activities like road marches and night infiltration courses. They march about 40 miles in those 54 hours."

It isn't long before the recruits are tired and hungry... but as they keep going they realize they can call on reserves they never knew they had. "Some of these recruits do things they never thought they could do," he said. "Some of them come from middle-class homes where everything has been handed to them. Others come from poorer homes where nothing was ever expected of them. If they finish the Crucible, they have accomplished something."

One recruit put it best. "I am going to finish this," he said. "And when I do, it will be the most positive thing I have done in my life."

Delta Company begins the Crucible at 3 a.m. with a six-mile road march from their barracks to Page Airfield, the Crucible site. Once there, recruits -- and that's the only thing the drill instructors call the trainees -- place their gear in huts and prepare for the first of four four-hour events.

Each event has a number of "warrior stations" each team of recruits must work together to overcome or solve. Each station is named for a Marine hero and the drill instructor has a recruit read a brief explanation of how the hero's actions exemplify the Corps and its values.

"I choose a different leader for each station. That way, all the recruits understand what it's like to be the leader and what they have to do to be a follower,... "For some of them, they want to run everything. They can't admit that a recruit who may not have been the sharpest in previous training has a good idea. Sometimes it's the quiet one who has the idea and no one will listen.

"You see the team learn as they go along," he continued. "At the beginning, they just charge ahead without a plan and without asking if anyone has an idea. By the end of the Crucible you see them working together better, getting advice from all team members and solving more of the problems."

Psalms 89:34 *My covenant will I not break, nor alter the thing that is gone out of my lips.*

One warrior station, for example, is built around an enemy-mined rope bridge that the recruits must cross with their gear and ammunition boxes. They have only a couple of short ropes and their personal gear to solve the problem. At another event, recruits run into firing positions and engage pop-up targets with 10 rounds in two magazines. Recruit teams battle each other with pugil sticks in yet another event.

The recruits grab food and water when they can. After the first two events comes a five-mile night march. "The night march was the toughest thing we've done here," said 18-year-old Pfc. Josh Lunceford of Charleston, W.Va. "The whole company went on it and whoever led it set a real fast pace. You couldn't see very well and people were tripping over stuff, and everyone was tired."

The recruits hit the rack for four hours of sleep, then begin another day and finish the final two events. "On the second day they are tired and hungry and it really starts to show," said Capt. John H. Rochford, Delta Company commander. "They start getting short with one another, but they realize after the first day they have to work together to finish. No one gets through the Crucible alone."

At the end of the second day, the recruits go through a night infiltration course and then hit the rack for another four hours. When they get up, they face a nine-mile march and the end of the Crucible.

The march begins at 4 a.m. and, at first, is done quietly. Recruits limp along, because no one wants to drop out this close to the end....

As the sun rises, the recruits cross DI Bridge. Once across, the drill instructors start Jody calls and the recruits join in. As they get closer to the main base, the Jody calls get louder until they reach the Parade Deck. The recruits form up around a half-size replica of the Marine Corps Memorial -- also known as the Iwo Jima Memorial. There, a significant transformation takes place.

"We're not just giving them basic training, we're turning them into Marines," Rochford said. "There's more to being a Marine than knowing how to fire a weapon. There's a whole tradition behind it, and we want these recruits to measure up to the men and women who went before them."

A colour guard raises the flag on the memorial. The chaplain reads a prayer specifically written for the finish of the Crucible, and the company first sergeant addresses the recruits. Then the drill instructors present each of their recruits with the Marine Corps insignia -- the eagle, globe and anchor. He shakes their hands and calls them "Marine" for the first time. Many accept the honour with tears streaming down their faces.

Psalms 89:34 *My covenant will I not break, nor alter the thing that is gone out of my lips.*

All that training, all that grilling, creates a Stand up, Marine. This means a Marine, whether on active duty, retired or veteran, always stand at attention during the playing of the Marines Hymn.

Age does not matter, rank does not matter – even under Rank Has Privileges profiling.

THIS IS ALSO OUR STORY. WE ARE HEAVEN'S STAND UP MARINES. We will always sing our song, Marching to Zion. We will not sit; we will always stand at attention, for our God and for Godliness.

One training session for the marines in the military recorded the following episode:

The trainee marines had been left to train in very bad weather in the winter. They dug fox holes to keep warm, but the weather still kept soaking their bocts and numbing their limbs.

These trainee marines kept training, because they had been told, one day about such a time, the helicopters will come and pick you up. You only need to be at the right place.

The trainee marines were given the co-ordinates of the pick-up point. The trainee marines were there on time, but the helicopters did not come.

A day went by and another. They were cold and hungry, they were thirsty and blistered. They had cold sores on their mouths and they were tired.

The trainee marines knew one thing, it did not matter how long the wait took, they just knew, perhaps another hour perhaps another half day, perhaps one more night, but they were going to go home.

Because they were hungry and their rations had been finished long before, and they just had a match to light a fire, they took the dishes, the pots and the pans, that they had used in their last proper meal, and filled them with the snow. When the snow melted, they shared the water, a sip at a time, for everyone.

The trainee marines had to survive the weather, they had to survive the wait.

Soon after, they heard the sound of the helicopter, and they knew they would be home.

The marines trusted their commanders. We trust high heaven, we trust God, the Creator of the Universe, the Giver of Life.

The trainee marines were rewarded with beef and chicken burgers and coca colas. If they wanted hot tea and coffee they got it. What of heaven, what of heaven?

Psalms 89:34 *My covenant will I not break, nor alter the thing that is gone out of my lips.*

We are yet to see, for the word of God says, we will only know, when we get there.

The "delay" does not matter. We will reap, in due season.

Revelation 1:18 says *I am he that liveth, and was dead; and, behold, I am alive for evermore, Amen; and have the keys of hell and of death.*

And Paul says to the Galatians in **Galatians 6:9** *And let us not be weary in well doing: for in due season we shall reap, if we faint not.*

The Bible says in **Jeremiah 29:***11 For I know the thoughts that I think toward you, saith the LORD, thoughts of peace, and not of evil, to give you an expected end. [12] Then shall ye call upon me, and ye shall go and pray unto me, and I will hearken unto you. [13] And ye shall seek me, and find me, when ye shall search for me with all your heart. [14] And I will be found of you, saith the LORD: and I will turn away your captivity, and I will gather you from all the nations, and from all the places whither I have driven you, saith the LORD; and I will bring you again into the place whence I caused you to be carried away captive.*

And in **2 Chronicles 7:14** *If my people, which are called by my name, shall humble themselves, and pray, and seek my face, and turn from their wicked ways; then will I hear from heaven, and will forgive their sin, and will heal their land.*

The United States Marines are good, in fact very good. But we have a Great Contender, the author and finisher of our faith.

The Marines have their drill, their confidence courses, their physical, marksmanship, field firing training. The marines have combat water survival training, and they even have crucible training and family days.

All they do, they just took from God's book of the law – the book Joshua read, the book Joshua kept. The Great Contender, the commander of the armies of heaven, led and leads from the front.

The Great Contender is on our side. He is not Napoleon Bonaparte, because Napoleon only led the French and defended France; He is not General S. Patton, who led in the invasion of Normandy on D-Day, or the generals who commanded more than 11 million troops of the Russian Red Army, by the end of World War 2.

He is not even Winston Churchill, who was proud to be called the Defender of Democracy.

Winston Churchill would tell the **world** that Britain would stand firm: "We shall defend our Island, whatever the cost may be; we shall fight on the beaches, we shall fight on the landing grounds, we shall fight in the fields and in the streets, we shall fight in the hills; we shall never surrender."

Psalms 89:34 *My covenant will I not break, nor alter the thing that is gone out of my lips.*

Bbc.co.uk. (2014). *Winston Churchill: Defender of Democracy.* [online]. Available at: http://www.bbc.co.uk/history/worldwars/wwtwo/churchill_defende r_01.shtml [Accessed 2018]

Winston Churchill would fight the Battle of Britain, one of the most gruelling battles of World War 2, but he would retreat at Dunkirk.

The "man" Joshua saw is the commander of everything and everyone man ever saw and will ever see, man included. He is the commander of the host of heaven. He is a Great Contender.

━━━━━━━━━ *Chapter 12* ━━━━━━━━━

Learn Of Me

Jesus is our example, in everything, and every time.

Jesus says in Matthew 11:29 *Take my yoke upon you, and **learn of me; for I am meek and lowly in heart:** and ye shall find rest unto your souls.*

The best we can do, is ask, what really did Jesus do, and how did He do what He did? The first thing that comes to my mind is: -

Jesus Prayed

The Bible says in **Mathew 26:36-41**, *Then cometh Jesus with them unto a place called Gethsemane, and saith*

---

*Psalms **89:34** My covenant will I not break, nor alter the thing that is gone out of my lips.*

unto the disciples, Sit ye here, while I go and pray yonder.

This is huge, this is massive. Jesus was and is the Son of God, and He does not carry that name on His shoulders, He prefers to be amongst us and be like us.

He goes yonder to pray.

And **Mathew 26: 37** says *And he took with him Peter and the two sons of Zebedee, and began to be sorrowful and very heavy. ³⁸ Then saith he unto them, My soul is exceeding sorrowful, even unto death: tarry ye here, and watch with me.*

Jesus felt the burden of sin even before He hung on the cross. Jesus was not sorrowful because He was afraid of the cross, He was sorrowful because you and I needed to watch with Him, but we never did.

Jesus was going to face a bruising battle, but He could handle it. The Father was sure the Son could handle it, but the disciples would stummer, they would run. Jesus had to pray for them too.

Jesus had taken responsibility of the disciples, and He knew it was going to be bad. Not many were going to stand. Jesus was burdened. He loved them so. He agonized for and over them. How could He leave them at a time like this, when Peter was still Peter, and the sons of Zebedee were still the sons of thunder? How could He?

Jesus had to go to the Father. He had to tell His Father, He had to ask His Father – if possible – let this cup pass. But the Father assured, you will be just ok. I will be there, in the earthquake and in the darkness too.

Mathew, in **26: 39** reports *And he went a little farther, and fell on his face, and prayed, saying, O my Father, if it be possible, let this cup pass from me: nevertheless not as I will, but as thou wilt.*

This prayer, this salutation in prayer, *Oh my Father*, is not done when all is well. It is a cry for help. It is supplication, a plea, a request, a petition.

Mathew 26: 40 says *And he cometh unto the disciples, and findeth them asleep, and saith unto Peter, What, could ye not watch with me one hour? [41] Watch and pray, that ye enter not into temptation: the spirit indeed is willing, but the flesh is weak.*

The disciples could not watch with and for Jesus. Jesus then said to His disciples, watch and pray for yourselves.

Jesus knew they had to pray. He had prayed for them, but they still had to pray for themselves. This is how we ought to live, watching and praying.

Watch that doors that should be closed are closed, watch that your mouth is guarded, watch who you choose as friends, watch how you walk, watch what you eat, watch watch watch!

Psalms 89:34 *My covenant will I not break, nor alter the thing that is gone out of my lips.*

The Bible says in **John 12:27-29** *Now is my soul troubled; and what shall I say? Father, save me from this hour: but for this cause came I unto this hour. ²⁸* *Father, glorify thy name. Then came there a voice from heaven, saying, I have both glorified it, and will glorify it again. ²⁹ The people therefore, that stood by, and heard it, said that it thundered: others said, An angel spake to him.*

Jesus prays, ***Father, save me from this hour: but for this cause came I unto this hour.*** Jesus's prayer is selfless. He acknowledges He has come to THE Hour, the day of reckoning. But that was not the important thing – it was the cause. What led Him to that hour was more important than the hour. You were the cause, I was the cause.

Jesus knew the importance and the weight of prayer. Jesus chose to pray alone. A crowd demands a crowd prayer. A personal prayer, a plea, a petition to your Father, demands that you go one on one with the Father.

It is not a prayer for attention, it is a prayer for strength, and it is a needy prayer. This kind of prayer means you need to take a step further. We need wisdom, even to know how we ought to pray.

Jesus prayed everywhere – in the desert, on mountain tops and at sea sides. Jesus kept connected with heaven, with His Father.

Jesus was spiritual, and faith connects with faith, and spirit with spirit.

The crowd does not and will never know your mission or vision. Neither can we depend on the prayers from the crowd. If that is all you can do, then please sleep, but at your peril.

When you understand the need and weight of prayer, you also pray before problems come. The Gethsemane prayer could not do whilst Jesus was hanging on the cross. It had to be done before Calvary, before the high priests, the scribes and the Pharisees came, it had to be prayed before.

The cross would demand, it would require a different type of prayer. Gethsemane was done. Jesus had to pray *Father, Father why have you forsaken me?* The Father had not forsaken His Son, the Father and the Son are one. Godliness was on the cross, so the world could see, what Godliness does and how it does what it does. Sacrifice. Calvary was a love sacrifice!

When the Psalmist wrote in **Psalms 22,** Jesus was there. **Jesus referred back to the word, His word,** *My God, my God, why hast thou forsaken me? why art thou so far from helping me, and from the words of my roaring? [2] O my God, I cry in the day time, but thou hearest not; and in the night season, and am not silent. [3] But thou art*

Psalms 89:34 *My covenant will I not break, nor alter the thing that is gone out of my lips.*

holy, O thou that inhabitest the praises of Israel. ⁴ *Our*
fathers trusted in thee: they trusted, and thou didst
deliver them. ⁵ *They cried unto thee, and were delivered:*
they trusted in thee, and were not confounded. ⁶ *But I am*
a worm, and no man; a reproach of men, and despised
of the people. ⁷ ***All they that see me laugh me to scorn:***
they shoot out the lip, they shake the head, saying, ⁸ ***He***
trusted on the LORD ***that he would deliver him: let him***
deliver him, seeing he delighted in him.

This was happening. The way David wrote it, thousands
of years earlier, Jesus remembered; it was His word. It
was His word fulfilled.

This kind of prayer, the disciples could not help Him
pray. He was alone. Jesus did not even expect them to
pray that kind of prayer. It was His cup, and the story
had been written – just for Him, by Him.

Yes, Jesus knew who would pray what prayer, and
when. There are times we also need to pray, for those
that should be praying for us. Jesus did.

He prayed for Peter, He prayed for all of them.
Regardless of how much we pray, sweat or no sweat,
there are cups that we have to drink, those cups cannot
just pass, because the cause is greater than the cup.

The sweat and the tears. There are tears that those that
pray for you may not understand. Those that pray with
you will know. Even those that pray with you, the

Calvary prayer they cannot do, not for you, because it is just your cup.

God knows and understands every sweat drop and every tear drop; nothing goes unnoticed by our Creator!

John says in **Revelation 21:4**, *And God shall wipe away all tears from their eyes; and there shall be no more death, neither sorrow, nor crying, neither shall there be any more pain: for the former things are passed away.*

We need to be friends with Jesus, acquaint ourselves with Him, as **Job 22:21** says *[21] Acquaint now thyself with him, and be at peace: thereby good shall come unto thee.* Jesus sticks closer than a brother.

In **Mathew 26:45-46** the Bible says *[45] Then cometh he to his disciples, and saith unto them, Sleep on now, and take your rest: behold, the hour is at hand, and the Son of man is betrayed into the hands of sinners. [46] Rise, let us be going: behold, he is at hand that doth betray me.*

In our lives, there is a day called the last day. This day we prepare for – we pray. Jesus took time out, to pray for that hour, that last day.

Prayer makes everything reachable, doable. Prayer is saying, not everything is within my hands, but everything, by God's grace, is within my reach! Paul

---

Psalms 89:34 *My covenant will I not break, nor alter the thing that is gone out of my lips.*

says *I can do everything (all things) through Christ who strengthens me.* **Philippians 4:13**

When we pray, we are saying, we have the right to object but God has the right to overrule. God overruled Paul's request for healing and He did to Jesus in Gethsemane. Jesus had to drink the cup, for you and me. We were the cause.

When we pray, the Lord may not have regard of what we want, if the cause is greater.

Jesus would say in **John 6:38** *For I came down from heaven, not to do mine own will, but the will of him that sent me.*

God had already assured. In **Matthew 3:16-17** the Bible says *And Jesus, when he was baptized, went up straightway out of the water: and, lo, the heavens were opened unto him, and he saw the Spirit of God descending like a dove, and lighting upon him: [17] **And lo a voice from heaven, saying, This is my beloved Son, in whom I am well pleased.***

Jesus prayed. He prayed for Himself and He also prayed for me and He prayed for you. The Father was well pleased. Now you belong, and I belong. We are now sons of God, because Jesus prayed.

The thought made John happy, it makes me very happy. John says in **1 John 3** *Behold, what manner of love the*

Father hath bestowed upon us, that we should be called the sons of God: therefore the world knoweth us not, because it knew him not. [2] **Beloved, now are we the sons of God, and it doth not yet appear what we shall be: but we know that, when he shall appear, we shall be like him; for we shall see him as he is.** [3] **And every man that hath this hope in him purifieth himself, even as he is pure.**

It is because of that assurance, that we are confident, that when Jesus bids us come, we truly have a home, a heaven to go to. We can joyfully sing (by Isaac Watts)

Come, we that love the Lord,
And let our joys be known;
Join in a song with sweet accord,
And thus surround the throne.

Refrain:
We're marching to Zion,
Beautiful, beautiful Zion;
We're marching upward to Zion,
The beautiful city of God.

The sorrows of the mind
Be banished from the place;
Religion never was designed
To make our pleasures less.

Psalms 89:34 *My covenant will I not break, nor alter the thing that is gone out of my lips.*

Let those refuse to sing,
Who never knew our God;
But children of the heav'nly King
May speak their joys abroad.

The men of grace have found
Glory begun below;
Celestial fruits on earthly ground
From faith and hope may grow.

The hill of Zion yields
A thousand sacred sweets
Before we reach the heav'nly fields,
Or walk the golden streets.

Then let our songs abound,
And every tear be dry;
We're marching through Immanuel's ground
To fairer worlds on high.

Just pray more fervently and believe more fully. **James 5:16**

Jesus Stood in the Breach

Standing in the breach is knowing God and understanding man. It means being there so that man will know what God wants them to know.

Standing in the breach means sacrifice. It means interceding.

The Bible says in **Ezekiel 22:30** *And I sought for a man among them, that should make up the hedge, and stand in the gap before me for the land, that I should not destroy it: but I found none.*

The law we know, the testimony we have. We are capacitated, to stand in the breach. Standing for right, because the Father is with us.

In **Isaiah 40:31** the Bible recognizes that strength can just dissipate. We can just feel tired, burnt out. But God is faithful. He renews our strength, just like He said and does for the eagles, and we can fly again.

Standing in the breach is done by Godly people. Standing in the breach requires honest and earnest living, we cannot be frivolous in the way we live, and standing in the breach needs holy living. There is no controversy, there is no argument, there is no confusion. **John 16:7-13** says the Holy Spirit will let you know what is good.

People who stand in the breach are bold but broken. Moses did. One preacher said boldness without Jesus is bullying, and brokenness without Christ is timidity. Again we quote John, the Holy Spirit will let us know what is good.

Psalms 89:34 *My covenant will I not break, nor alter the thing that is gone out of my lips.*

The Bible says about Moses, in **Deuteronomy 5:5** *I stood between the LORD and you at that time, to shew you the word of the LORD: for ye were afraid by reason of the fire, and went not up into the mount;*

Moses was referring to this episode of Numbers. The Bible captures this conversation between Moses and his God –

Numbers 16:45 *Get you up from among this congregation, that I may consume them as in a moment. And they fell upon their faces. ⁴⁶ And Moses said unto Aaron, Take a censer, and put fire therein from off the altar, and put on incense, and go quickly unto the congregation, and make an atonement for them: for there is wrath gone out from the LORD; the plague is begun. ⁴⁷ And Aaron took as Moses commanded, and ran into the midst of the congregation; and, behold, the plague was begun among the people: and he put on incense, and made an atonement for the people. ⁴⁸ And he stood between the dead and the living; and the plague was stayed.*

It takes the bold and broken to stand in the gap, to connect the people of God with their God.

Jesus did. Jesus was not a Moses. Jesus was the Son of the Father. He stood in the breach for all people, for all time.

Jesus was Humble

Paul to the Philippians says – be humble, be moderate.

The Bible says in **Philippians 4:5-8** *Let your moderation be known unto all men. The Lord is at hand.* *[6] Be careful for nothing; but in every thing by prayer and supplication with thanksgiving let your requests be made known unto God. [7] And the peace of God, which passeth all understanding, shall keep your hearts and minds through Christ Jesus. [8] Finally, brethren, whatsoever things are true, whatsoever things are honest, whatsoever things are just, whatsoever things are pure, whatsoever things are lovely, whatsoever things are of good report; if there be any virtue, and if there be any praise, think on these things. [9] Those things, which ye have both learned, and received, and heard, and seen in me, do: and the God of peace shall be with you.*

God's word gives us sense. As long as we are anchored on Christ, we will not drift. The Holy Spirit will let us know what is good. When and where there is argument and confusion, the Holy Spirit of the Lord is just not there!

The Bible says in **Isaiah 57:15** *For thus saith the high and lofty One that inhabiteth eternity, whose name is Holy; I dwell in the high and holy place, with him also that is of a contrite and humble spirit, to revive the spirit*

Psalms 89:34 *My covenant will I not break, nor alter the thing that is gone out of my lips.*

of the humble, and to revive the heart of the contrite ones.

The Lord resists the proud. The Bible says in Ezekiel 17:24 *And all the trees of the field shall know that I the LORD have brought down the high tree, have exalted the low tree, have dried up the green tree, and have made the dry tree to flourish: I the LORD have spoken and have done it.*

Micah says *He hath shewed thee, O man, what is good; and what doth the LORD require of thee, but to do justly, and to love mercy, and to walk humbly with thy God?* **Micah 6:8,** and

Paul to the Colossians says *Put on therefore, as the elect of God, holy and beloved, bowels of mercies, kindness, humbleness of mind, meekness, longsuffering;* **Colossians 3:12**

James says *But he giveth more grace. Wherefore he saith, God resisteth the proud, but giveth grace unto the humble.* **James 4:6**

The testimony of Jesus speaks - humility.

Jesus Cared

Paul says in **Hebrews 4: 14** *Seeing then that we have a great high priest, that is passed into the heavens, Jesus the Son of God, let us hold fast our profession. [15] For we* have not an high priest which cannot be touched with the feeling of our infirmities; but was in all points tempted like as we are, yet without sin.

Paul is just summarizing the nature, the character of Jesus – He is touched by the feeling of our infirmities. He cares.

That is why Jesus says, as reported by Mathew, in **Matthew 25:31-46** *"When the Son of Man comes in his glory, and all the angels with him, he will sit on his throne in heavenly glory. All the nations will be gathered before him, and **he will separate the people one from another** as a shepherd separates the sheep from the goats. He will put the sheep on his right and the goats on his left. "Then the King will say to those on his right, 'Come, you who are blessed by my Father; take your inheritance, the kingdom prepared for you since the creation of the world. **For I was** hungry and you gave me something to eat, I was thirsty and you gave me something to drink, I was a stranger and you invited me in, **I needed** clothes and you clothed me, I was sick and you looked after me, I was in prison and you came to visit me.' "Then the righteous will answer him, 'Lord, **when did we see you** hungry and feed you, or thirsty and give you something to drink? When did we see you a stranger and invite you in, **or needing** clothes and clothe you? When did we see you sick or in prison and go to*

Psalms 89:34 *My covenant will I not break, nor alter the thing that is gone out of my lips.*

visit you?' "The King will reply, 'I tell you the truth, **whatever you did for one of the least of these brothers of mine, you did for me.'** *"Then he will say to those on his left, 'Depart from me, you who are cursed, into the eternal fire prepared for the devil and his angels. For I was hungry and you gave me nothing to eat, I was thirsty and you gave me nothing to drink, I was a stranger and you did not invite me in, I needed clothes and you did not clothe me, I was sick and in prison and you did not look after me.' "They also will answer, 'Lord, when did we see you hungry or thirsty or a stranger or needing clothes or sick or in prison, and did not help you?' "He will reply, 'I tell you the truth, whatever you did not do for one of the least of these, you did not do for me.' "Then they will go away to eternal punishment, but the righteous to eternal life."*

The good and the bad will ask the same question, when did we? Jesus will answer, **whatever you did for one of the least of these brothers of mine, you did for me.**

The commission and the omission will separate people. Jesus loves us, His brothers. With Jesus, we are all sons of the Father.

Jesus Did not Quit.

Jesus knew His mission. Even in His prayer He acknowledges it will be tough, the road to Calvary would be tough, but He never quit.

Micah 7:8 says *Rejoice not against me, O mine enemy: when I fall, I shall arise; when I sit in darkness, the LORD shall be a light unto me.*

It does not matter how low you get, how long and how deep the fall, rise.

People have a habit of spending time talking about the fall. The fall does not matter, the rise does.

Quit on sin, for any other will not take us to heaven.

Jesus said where he went the scribes and the Pharisees would not come. They needed to quit on sin and they needed to quit sinning.

Jesus said then and He is saying now – learn of me, learn from me.

======= **Chapter 13** =======

The Blood Covenant – *An Unchanging Covenant*

The Lord says through Jeremiah *And ye shall be my people, and I will be your God.* **Jeremiah 30:22.**

And in **Genesis 9:11-13** *And I will establish my covenant with you, neither shall all flesh be cut off any more by the waters of a flood; neither shall there anymore be a flood to destroy the earth. [12] And God said, This is the token of the covenant which I make between me and you and every living creature that is with you, for perpetual generations: [13] I do set my bow in the cloud, and it shall be for a token of a covenant between me and the earth.*

After Egypt the Lord says to the children of Israel in **Exodus 19:5** *Now therefore, if ye will obey my voice indeed, and keep my covenant, then ye shall be a peculiar treasure unto me above all people: for all the earth is mine:* And

The Bible says of Moses in **Exodus 34:28** *And he was there with the LORD forty days and forty nights; he did neither eat bread, nor drink water. And he wrote upon the tables the words of the covenant, the Ten Commandments.*

The Word of the Lord, this book, the Bible, is a book of eternal covenants.

Deuteronomy 4:13 says *And he declared unto you his covenant, which he commanded you to perform, even ten commandments; and he wrote them upon two tables of stone.....Know therefore that the LORD thy God, he is God, the faithful God, which keepeth covenant and mercy with them that love him and keep his commandments to a thousand generations;* **Deuteronomy 7:9** ..... *And the LORD, he it is that doth go before thee; he will be with thee, he will not fail thee, neither forsake thee: fear not, neither be dismayed.* **Deuteronomy 31:8**

Psalms 89:34 *My covenant will I not break, nor alter the thing that is gone out of my lips.*

David could say in **Psalm 103:17-18** *But the mercy of the LORD is from everlasting to everlasting upon them that fear him, and his righteousness unto children's children;* ¹⁸ *To such as keep his covenant, and to those that remember his commandments to do them.* And

Paul would say of Jesus in **Hebrews 8:6** *But now hath he obtained a more excellent ministry, by how much also he is the mediator of a better covenant, which was established upon better promises.....* **Hebrews 9:15** *And for this cause he is the mediator of the new testament, that by means of death, for the redemption of the transgressions that were under the first testament, they which are called might receive the promise of eternal inheritance.......* **Hebrews 12:24** *And to Jesus the mediator of the new covenant, and to the blood of sprinkling, that speaketh better things than that of Abel........* **Hebrews 13:20-21** *Now the God of peace, that brought again from the dead our Lord Jesus, that great shepherd of the sheep, through the blood of the everlasting covenant,* ²¹ *Make you perfect in every good work to do his will, working in you that which is well pleasing in his sight, through Jesus Christ; to whom be glory for ever and ever. Amen.*

Paul concludes in **1 Timothy 2:5** *For there is one God, and one mediator between God and men, the man Christ Jesus;*

In **Exodus 2: 23-25** the Bible says *And it came to pass in process of time, that the king of Egypt died: and the children of Israel sighed by reason of the bondage, and they cried, and their cry came up unto God by reason of the bondage. ²⁴ And God heard their groaning, and God remembered his covenant with Abraham, with Isaac, and with Jacob. ²⁵ And God looked upon the children of Israel, and God had respect unto them.*

It is not that God had forgotten. No, He does not. He creates conditions for us to call Him. When we call on the name of the Lord, the Lord hears, He remembers.

David says in **Psalms 103**, *God remembers that we are dust*. God cannot forget, he made everything about us, from the dust, and then He gave us breath – He cannot just forget. We are so precious God decided to fill us with His Holy Spirit, eternal Spirit, when we chose His Son, Jesus the Christ.

This is the Lord who says in **Psalm 89:34** *My covenant will I not break, nor alter the thing that is gone out of my lips.*

So God does not forget as we forget. How can He, He is God. He sets everything in motion, both in time and in space.

The Bible says He instructs the angels of heaven to look after us, He commands everything to stay in place, and

Psalms 89:34 *My covenant will I not break, nor alter the thing that is gone out of my lips.*

He is the one who created. He spoke and it was established, He commanded and it (everything) stood fast – so how can He forget?

Remembering is a language we understand. Man, by nature, is very forgetful. It is virtue to remember. The word of God uses the same word, so that we also understand.

Years after the children of Israel had been remembered and were led out of Egypt; they still would not listen or obey the commandments of God. It was a stop start generation.

Today they are there with God and in God, tomorrow they are not. So God also remembered, as David would say in **Psalms 103** – God remembered they were dust.

He remembered we would need a Saviour. Moses had done His part, so did Joshua, the Judges, the kings and all.

We needed someone bigger and better than Moses, or David or Solomon. We needed someone bigger and better than the prophets, someone bigger and better than the angels of heaven. We needed the Son of God.

We needed Jesus.

Isaiah then says in **9:6-7** *For unto us a child is born, unto us a son is given: and the government shall be upon his shoulder: and his name shall be called Wonderful,*

Counsellor, The mighty God, The everlasting Father, The Prince of Peace. [7] Of the increase of his government and peace there shall be no end, upon the throne of David, and upon his kingdom, to order it, and to establish it with judgment and with justice from henceforth even forever. The zeal of the LORD of hosts will perform this.

And when the fullness of time was come, Jesus came into the world. Paul believed that and so do we.

That is why Paul then says in **Acts 20:32** *And now, brethren, I commend you to God, and to the word of his grace, which is able to build you up, and to give you an inheritance among all them which are sanctified.*

We will have an inheritance, amoung all who are sanctified. The Lord sanctifies. He works on us, through His Holy Spirit, moment by moment so that we, too, remember that Jesus is the Son of God, Jesus is our Saviour, our Redeemer. Jesus is everything we will need, in time and place.

The instructions to the disciples had been clear – stay here until the Holy Spirit comes upon you.

The Bible says in **Acts 2** *And when the day of Pentecost was fully come, they were all with one accord in one place. [2] And suddenly there came a sound from heaven as of a rushing mighty wind, and it filled all the house*

Psalms 89:34 *My covenant will I not break, nor alter the thing that is gone out of my lips.*

where they were sitting. ³ And there appeared unto them cloven tongues like as of fire, and it sat upon each of them. ⁴ And they were all filled with the Holy Ghost

That Holy Spirit gave them power. Power to stand before the kings, the judges and the governors of Rome.

Power to challenge ungodly thinking. Power to challenge morality. Power to deliver from the ravages of sin, from demonic powers, from powers that reside in heavenly places.

God gave power to challenge foreign beliefs and foreign doctrine.

God gave power to think straight, power to challenge principalities, power to step on and crush snakes and scorpions, power to rebuke sin.

The Lord sent the power, by and through His Holy Spirit.

This is the Lord we worship. In **1 Samuel 7:10** the Bible says *And as Samuel was offering up the burnt offering, the Philistines drew near to battle against Israel: but the LORD thundered with a great thunder on that day upon the Philistines, and discomfited them; and they were smitten before Israel.*

The Lord had instructed that incense was burned daily on the altar, at the time of the morning and the evening sacrifices.

The incense was specific, and the instructions were clear. Samuel was doing what God had instructed to do, when the Philistines came.

The Philistines were not going to be allowed to disturb the offering of the offering. Samuel had and was going to finish what he was doing. Samuel was not doing it only for himself, He was the priest, He was doing it for himself and for the whole house of Israel, the whole congregation, even the mixed multitude.

So Samuel could not be disturbed, he still had to sweep the coals from the alter of burnt offerings. He still had to throw the ashes away. So how could he be disturbed? Samuel still needed to light another fire, at the next offering.

The Bible says *The LORD thundered from heaven, and the most High uttered his voice.* **2 Samuel 22:14**

This is the Lord Job describes in **Job 37:4-5**. The Bible says *After it a voice roareth: he thundereth with the voice of his excellency; and he will not stay them when his voice is heard.*
[5] God thundereth marvellously with his voice; great things doeth he, which we cannot comprehend.

Psalms 89:34 *My covenant will I not break, nor alter the thing that is gone out of my lips.*

David could then say in **Psalm 18:3** *I will call upon the* LORD, *who is worthy to be praised: so shall I be saved from mine enemies.*

Not everyone who hears the roar knows what it means. Spiritual things are spiritually discerned. **John says in 12:29** *The people therefore, that stood by, and heard it, said that it thundered: others said, An angel spake to him.*

The Lord roars for His own, He will not remain silent. He is a covenant keeper.

He says in **John 14:1-3** *"Do not let your hearts be troubled. Trust in God; trust also in me. In my Father's house are many rooms; if it were not so, I would have told you. I am going there to prepare a place for you. And if I go and prepare a place for you, I will come back and take you to be with me that you also may be where I am.*

This is Jesus. His sayings are true. He will keep His covenant, for the Lord God, His Father has given Him a name above every other name. Jesus was and is the ultimate sacrifice. Jesus is not an option, He is not an alternative, He is the only one - there was and there is just no other.

The Bible says in **Acts 4:12** *Neither is there salvation in any other: for there is none other name under heaven given among men, whereby we must be saved.*

What is washed is saved. It is not known that anyone can wash and throw away. The cleaning is for saving. This is the way that our God works.

In **1 John 1:7** the Bible says *But if we walk in the light, as he is in the light, we have fellowship one with another, and the blood of Jesus Christ his Son cleanseth us from all sin*

Even David knew this, if clean, then he is also saved. He prays, *Wash me thoroughly from mine iniquity, and cleanse me from my sin.* **Psalm 51:2**

The Lord says through Isaiah, *Come now, and let us reason together, saith the LORD: though your sins be as scarlet, they shall be as white as snow; though they be red like crimson, they shall be as wool.* **Isaiah 1:18**

Only the Creator, could have loved the way God loved, only Jesus could have endured the cross the way Jesus did, only Jesus could have prayed the way Jesus prayed.

Heaven's protocol respects covenants. It is never easy, trouble will always come. It is just better with Jesus.

There are many enemies, but we are never without a friend, Jesus is His name

Jesus, is a covenant keeper.

***Psalms* 89:34** *My covenant will I not break, nor alter the thing that is gone out of my lips.*

Conclusion

The Bible is the sure word of God. This Bible says heaven is not for the fearful but the faithful, heaven is not for the compromising, but for the sympathizing.

The children of Israel, all of them, walked under the cloud, all crossed the red sea, all ate manna, all drank from the rock, but only a few of those who did, got into the promised land.

Some, who did not cross the red sea or drink from the rock, did get into Canaan. Going to heaven is not a function of what we ate and how we ate it, even though what we eat and how we eat, is important. It is not premised on which rivers and seas we crossed and how, even though the rivers and seas we cross and how we cross them is important. Going to heaven is about Godliness.

The Holy Spirit of God will tell us what to do, when and how. When we have done right, we know it.

Like Job, we ought to say, regardless of everything against us, WE WILL SEE GOD. We are calm, we shake off the dust and we move on.

The way we do things, sitting, walking, standing, is a reflection of where we are going. We exist within time and space, but relate to our God who is outside time, outside space, yet so conscious of time, so conscious of space.

Our God says in **Isaiah 46:9** *Remember the former things of old: for I am God, and there is none else; I am God, and there is none like me,*

This is the Lord of our lives; this is the God we worship. There is none like Him.

There is nothing better, than walking in the direction where love, joy, peace, goodness, and everything Godly, is found – the Holy Highway. The Gaither Vocal Band sang -

There's a road called the holy highway that once was a desert land
Very soon you'll hear the sound of a holy marching band
Everlasting joy upon them, there's a remnant strong and true
We bring the song back to Zion; we bring the praise back to you

We exalt You, God Almighty, You are worthy to be praised
Let all nations bow before You, Holy Ancient of all days

There's a road called the holy highway, where the people dance and shout
For the enemy is running with confusion all about
Raise our banners in the victory; raise them high His word is true
We bring our song back to Zion, we bring the praise back to you

Psalms 89:34 *My covenant will I not break, nor alter the thing that is gone out of my lips.*

We exalt You, God Almighty, You are worthy to be praised
Let all nations bow before You, Holy Ancient of all days

Holy, holy, holy, Lord God Almighty
Holy, holy holy is the Lord
Hallelujah, hallelujah, hallelujah
Hallelujah, hallelujah, hallelujah

There's a road called the holy highway that once was a desert land
Very soon you'll hear the sound of a holy marching band and
Everlasting joy upon them, there's a remnant strong and true
We bring the song back to Zion; we bring the praise back to you
We bring the praise back to you

Songwriters: Virginia M Hendricks - Gaither Vocal Band, Ernie Haase & Signature Sound

The Lord says in **John 6:37**...*and the one who comes to Me, I will certainly not cast out.*

It is not in vain that we worship God: **Jesus Is Coming Back!**

***Psalms* 89:34** *My covenant will I not break, nor alter the thing that is gone out of my lips.*

REFERENCES

Bbc.co.uk. (2014). *Winston Churchill: Defender of Democracy.*
[online]. Available at:
http://www.bbc.co.uk/history/worldwars/wwtwo/churchill_defende
r_01.shtml [Accessed 2018]

Johnson S., Sciencing.com (April 24, 2018)., . *How Does Water
Affect Sound?* [online]. Available at:
https://sciencing.com/water-affect-sound-8510076.html   [January
2019]

Touregypt.net. (1996-2019). *Mount Sinai (and the peak of Mount
Musa or Mousa).* [online].
Available at:
http://www.touregypt.net/featurestories/mountsinai.htm [Accessed
February 22, 2019]

Wikipedia.org. (January, 2019). *Mount Sinai 9.* [online]. Available
at: https://en.wikipedia.org/wiki/Mount_Sinai 9
[Accessed February 22, 2019]

Wikipedia.org. (July, 2018). *Woes of the Pharisees.* [online].
Available at
https://en.m.wikipedia.org/wiki/Woes_of_the_Pharisees [Accessed
February 23, 2019]

OTHER BOOKS BY THE AUTHOR:

- CHAPTERS OF CHRISTIAN LIFE

- ALONE WITH GOD IN 22 STEPS
  - Proverbs 31-

- THE LORD OUR HABITATION

- THE LOST DRACHMA
  - Love -

- PHARAOH'S HORSES AND HIS CHARIOTS

- A TESTIMONY OF OUR FAITH